PUB WALKS

East

C000182106

Other areas covered in the Pub Walks series include:

Bedfordshire
Berkshire
Bristol & Bath
Buckinghamshire
Cheshire
The Chilterns
Cornwall Coast Path
The Cotswolds
The Cotswold Way
North & West Cumbria
South Cumbria
Dartmoor and South Devon
Derbyshire
Devon
Dorset Coast Path
East Sussex
Essex
West Essex
Exmoor & North Devon
Gloucestershire
Hampshire
Herefordshire
Hertfordshire
Lancashire
Leicestershire and Rutland
Lincolnshire
Middlesex and West London

Hampshire and New Forest
Norfolk
North London
Northamptonshire
Nottinghamshire
Oxfordshire
The Ridgeway
Shropshire
Somerset
South Downs
Staffordshire
Suffolk
Surrey
Surrey Hills
East Sussex
West Sussex
The Thames Valley
The Thames Path
Warwickshire
Wayfarer's Walk
Wiltshire
Worcestershire
East Yorkshire
North Yorkshire
South Yorkshire
West Yorkshire

A complete catalogue is available from the publisher at
3 Catherine Road, Newbury, Berkshire.

P U B W A L K S
I N
East Yorkshire

FORTY CIRCULAR WALKS
AROUND EAST YORKSHIRE INNS

Leonard Markham

COUNTRYSIDE BOOKS
NEWBURY, BERKSHIRE

First Published 1994
© Leonard Markham 1994
Reprinted with revisions 2002

All rights reserved. No reproduction
permitted without the prior permission
of the publishers:

COUNTRYSIDE BOOKS
3 Catherine Road
Newbury, Berkshire

ISBN 1 85306 270 7

Publisher's Note

Designed by Mon Mohan
Cover illustration by Colin Doggett
Photographs by the Author
Maps drawn by Ian Streets

Produced through MRM Associates Ltd., Reading
Printed in England

Contents

Introduction   7

Walk   1   Rudston: The Bosville Arms (½ mile)   9

       2   North Cave: The White Hart (1 mile)   12

       3   Hull: Ye Olde White Harte (1½ miles)   15

       4   Hedon: The King's Head (1¾ miles)   18

       5   Beverley: The Monk's Walk (2 miles)   21

       6   Foston on the Wolds: The Plough (2½ miles)   25

       7   Harpham: The St Quintin Arms (2½ miles)   28

       8   Burton Pidsea: The Nancy (3 miles)   31

       9   Blacktoft: The Hope and Anchor (3 miles)   33

      10   Driffield: The Bell (1 mile)   36

      11   Patrington: The Hildyard Arms (3 miles)   39

      12   Holmpton: The George and Dragon (3 miles)   42

      13   Bishop Wilton: The Fleece (6 miles)   45

      14   Burton Agnes: The Blue Bell (3½ miles)   48

      15   Allerthorpe: The Plough Inn (4 miles)   51

      16   Newton upon Derwent: The Half Moon (4 miles)   53

      17   Old Ellerby: The Blue Bell (4¼ miles)   56

      18   Barmston: The Black Bull (4¼ miles)   59

      19   Huggate: The Wolds Inn (4½ miles)   62

      20   Seaton Ross: The Black Horse (4½ miles)   65

21   North Newbald: The Tiger (4½ miles)   68

22   Roos: The Roos Arms (4½ miles)   71

23   Skidby: The Half Moon (4½ miles)   74

24   South Cave: The Fox and Coney (4½ miles)   77

25   Millington: The Gate Inn (5 miles)   80

26   Lund: The Wellington Inn (5½ miles)   83

27   Little Weighton: The Black Horse (5½ miles)   86

28   Fangfoss: The Carpenter's Arms (6 miles)   89

29   Hornsea: The Rose and Crown (6 miles)   92

30   Holme on Spalding Moor: The Blacksmith
      Arms (6 miles)   95

31   Easington: The Granby (6 miles)   98

32   Market Weighton: The Londesborough Arms
      Hotel (6 miles)   101

33   Wetwang: The Black Swan (6 miles)   105

34   Bempton: The White Horse (6½ miles)   108

35   Stamford Bridge: The Swordsman (7 miles)   111

36   Flamborough: The Royal Dog and Duck (7 miles) 114

37   Laxton: The Bricklayer's Arms (8 miles)   117

38   Brantingham: The Triton (8 miles)   120

39   Bielby: The College Arms (8 miles)   123

40   Kilnsea: The Crown and Anchor (8½ miles)   126

Introduction

Tranquil towns and villages, rolling chalk hills and dry valleys, towering cliffs and gentle beaches and a scimitared spit as remote as many a highland glen. This is East Yorkshire, which to those legislators who in the early 1970s swept away 1,000 years of history with the scratch of a pen, was deemed to be part of Humberside. To the rest of us who campaigned so hard for a reversal of the treachery, it always has been, and still is, East Yorkshire. What a jaunty, kite-shaped county! Tie your string on Spurn Point and we will have some capital sport, ranging over an area unrivalled in all England.

First a word on practicalities. The sketch map which accompanies each walk is designed to give a simple yet accurate idea of the route to be followed. For those who prefer a more detailed map, the relevant number in the OS Landranger 1:50 000 series is also given. Please remember the Country Code and make sure gates are not left open or any farm animals disturbed.

No special equipment is needed to enjoy the countryside on foot, but do wear a stout pair of shoes and remember that at least one muddy patch is likely even on the sunniest day. Do please also remember that even the most accommodating of inn landlords is unlikely to welcome walkers with muddy boots, and leave yours outside the pub when you return.

Many of the walks in this book recommend leaving your car in the inn car park, with the intention of eating and drinking at the inn on your return. If you do so, particularly outside normal opening hours, please ask the landlord's permission. A car left for hours in an otherwise empty car park may become an object of suspicion.

So, what can the footloose inn-goer expect in this boot and bar selection? The breath of solitude. Wind tans. Exhilarating views and 40 varied routes, centred on 40 of the area's finest inns.

Leonard Markham
Spring 2002

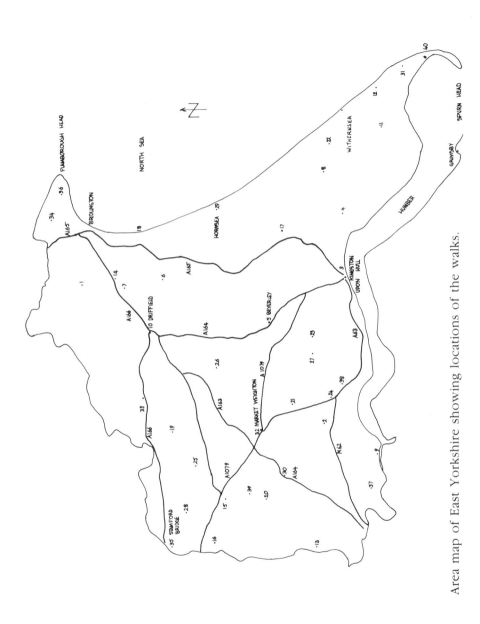

Area map of East Yorkshire showing locations of the walks.

Rudston
The Bosville Arms

In cloning old coaching inns, brewing companies can be as rapacious as old-time body snatchers, tearing the souls from some of our best loved wayside halts. So thank goodness for the free-housers – entrepreneurs like those in the Bosville Arms who have thoroughly modernised a village institution without altering its character one jot. Created by a subtle marriage of brickwork and stained glass, the ambience is bright, lively and plush. The quality decorations in the restaurant, lounge bar and taproom (too common a description for a facility this attractive) include a gallery of autographed photographs of film stars. Who else remembers Jean Peters and Jack Palance? The ultimate approval of the conversion works comes from a former landlord, Kit Scuffam, who has a reserved seat in the taproom.

The inn serves standard bar and restaurant fare, including Sunday lunch. The choices are, typically, steak pie, roast chicken, gammon, lasagne, and various salads and vegetarian dishes. All-day breakfasts and afternoon teas are a speciality. Children are welcome for meals. The house ales are John Smith's and Black Sheep, with Miller's and Becks lagers, Strongbow cider and draught Guinness. The inn has six en suite letting bedrooms and an inviting children's play area/picnic

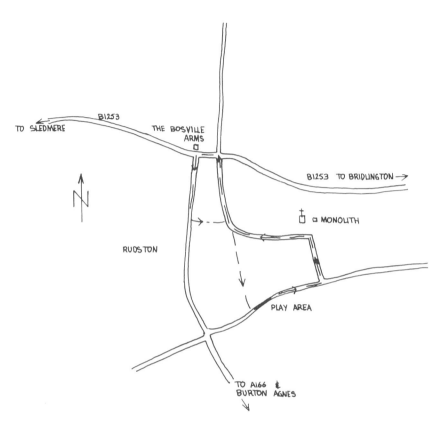

lawn to the side.

Opening times during the summer months are 11 am to 11 pm daily (Sundays 12 noon to 10.30 pm). During the winter, opening times are Monday to Thursday 11 am to 3 pm and 7 pm to 11 pm; Friday 11 am to 3 pm and 5 pm to 11 pm – Saturdays 11 am to 11 pm and Sundays 12 noon to 10.30 pm.

Telephone: 01262 420259.

How to get there: The inn is on the roadside (B1253), 5 miles west of Bridlington.

Parking: Park in the inn car park.

Length of the walk: ½ mile. OS Map Landranger series 101 (inn GR 095678).

10

A lazy back lanes parlour-slippers tour of the pretty village of Rudston. Midway there is a well-equipped play area for the children. For antiquarians, the church of All Saints and the brooding 4,000-year-old Rudston Monolith, in its churchyard, are full of interest.

The Walk

Go straight forward from the inn along Long Street. Bear left after 150 yards on a metalled footpath, cross a ditch on a pedestrian bridge and bear right to a road. Turn right on Middle Street and keep right past Waterside House, swinging left at the side of the village hall and the recreation ground, along Marton Lane.

At the next junction turn left on Church Lane, walking on to the church. Inside you can read the fascinating story of a local farmer who in April 1933 uncovered a splendid mosaic pavement with his plough – it had lain only 18 inches beneath the soil for over 1,600 years.

Turn left on School Lane and turn right on Middle Street to the main road. Turn left for a short distance, back to the inn.

Other local attractions: Scenic drive along the length of the B1253 from Sledmere to Bridlington.

2 North Cave
The White Hart

Dating from 1773, this one-time coaching inn is full of character. A blast on the posting horn for the eccentricities of the English inn and hurrah for original beams, ultrawide doorways (to aid the passage of crinolined ladies), open fires with brass hoods and a menu whose 'home-made' pronouncements even extend to the chips.

The White Hart has an unspoilt, unaltered taproom (spot the unusual clock) and three comfortable best rooms. The traditional menu is supplemented by vegetarian options such as moussaka, wheat and walnut casserole and Italian broccoli and cream cheese pie and by daily specials. Mainstays are grilled steaks, steak and kidney pie, minced beef and mushroom pie, chicken supreme, gammon and pineapple, fish pie and haddock fillet. The specials board lists, for example, beef hotpot, cottage pie and chicken chasseur. Sunday lunches are a speciality. Children are welcome for meals. The hand-pulled real ales are Mansfield Riding Bitter and Mansfield Mild. The alternatives are Foster's and McEwan lagers and draught Guinness.

Opening times are Monday to Saturday 12 noon to 3 pm and 5 pm to 11 pm. Sunday hours are 12 noon to 10.30 pm.

Telephone: 01430 422432.

12

How to get there: The inn is in the village of North Cave, north-west of Hull (off junction 38 of the M62).

Parking: Park in the inn car park.

Length of the walk: 1 mile. OS Map Landranger series 106 (inn GR 893325).

A short streamside saunter. The picturesque cottages, complete with resident ducks and drakes, bring to mind 'There's an old mill by the stream, Nellie Dean'.

The Walk
Turn left from the inn on Westgate and walk on to the bend. Bear left on Appleton Lane and turn right on Church Street, continuing towards the church of All Saints. Turn left at the side of the church and go left, following the public footpath sign, along the side of a pretty stream. Continue on a raised footpath, following the stream down to a kissing gate, and turn right, admiring the charming old mill pool. Continue along the path and go left on the street for about ¼ mile.

Go left again opposite a house called Pathways, following a public footpath marker back over the stream on a footbridge. Continue along Mill Lane and, at the top, turn right along Church Street, going right over the bridge on Blossom Lane and turning immediately left,

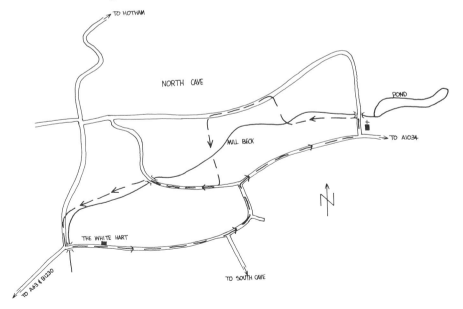

following the public footpath sign alongside the stream. Bear left on the lane and, at the junction, turn left along Westgate, back to the inn.

Other local attractions: The church of All Saints (spacious and impressive interior with striking nave arcades and alabaster monuments from the time of King James I).

14

3 Hull
Ye Olde White Harte

Ye Olde White Harte has been miraculously preserved for over four centuries in the aspic of Hull's expansion. Two lavishly carved, oak-panelled downstairs bars, the colour of Guinness, inglenooked fireplaces and old weapons create a 17th century time warp. Ye Olde White Harte was almost certainly the residence of Hull's governor, Sir

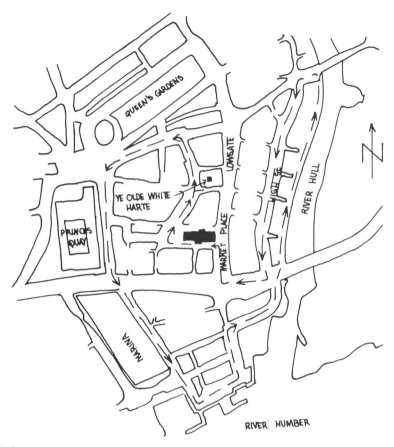

John Hotham, and one of his first-floor chambers, today known as the 'Plotting Parlour', is said to have been the meeting place for the Parliamentarian cabal whose refusal to allow Charles I entry into Hull in 1642 sparked the English Civil War. The chamber and the adjacent room today form the highly atmospheric restaurant.

Anything other than proper English 'vittles' would break the period spell and Ye Olde White Harte obliges in a satisfyingly traditional menu. Try the girding bar meals, such as mince and dumpling, beef in ale pie, corn beef hash, toad-in-the-hole, Yorkshire pudding and roast beef, jam roly-poly, apple crumble and bread-and-butter pudding. The restaurant fare includes home-made soup, mixed grill, gammon and beef steaks and trout. Children are welcome in the restaurant. The inn also has a courtyard beer garden.

The range of real hand-pulled ales are what your sword arm's for,

16

so raise your tankards for Younger No. 3, IPA and XB, Theakston Old Peculier, and Newcastle Exhibition and Export. The alternative brews are Becks and McEwan lagers, and draught Guinness.

Opening times are Monday to Saturday 11 am to 11 pm. Sunday hours are 12 noon to 10.30 pm.

Telephone: 01482 326363.

How to get there: The inn is flanked by Silver Street and Bowlalley Lane (accessed from both), east of High Street and the River Hull.

Parking: A choice of 'pay and display' parking is available close by.

Length of the walk: 1½ miles. OS Map Landranger series 107 (inn GR 100287).

A really absorbing Old Town amble which for atmosphere and historical interest can compete with any other town trails in northern England.

The Walk

Turn left from the inn along Silver Street and go right along the street known as the Land of Green Ginger. Continue on Manor Street and bear left on Alfred Gelder Street. Go left again alongside the exposed viewing area at Beverley Gate and walk beside the Princes Quay development.

Cross the busy main A63 road (use the crossing facilities) and continue at the side of the marina on Humber Dock Street. Go left on the River Humber frontage on Nelson Street, then turn left again down Queen Street. Go right on Humber Street, swing left by the Tidal Surge Barrier and just before the Myton Road bridge go right on Rotenhering Staith, bearing left under the road bridge on to a walkway at the side of the River Hull.

Continue on a boardwalk and go left at the next bridge and left again down High Street. Turn right and then right again, passing by the gilded statue of 'King Billy' (William III) and go left alongside Holy Trinity church. Turn right, and go right again, back to the inn.

Other local attractions: Visitors could spend a whole day in High Street alone. Its Ye Olde Black Boy is another of my favourite pubs and Wilberforce House, the adjacent Hull Museum of Transport and Hull and East Riding Museum, a little down the way (free entry to each), are all really fascinating. Come another day to explore the Town Docks Museum (history of the fishing industry), the Spurn Lightship, anchored in the marina, the Ferens Art Gallery and Holy Trinity church.

Hedon
The King's Head

Hedon was a thriving port when Hull was but a twinkle in Neptune's eye. A historic town dominated by the soaring presence of St Augustine's church – the King of Holderness – it once had 13 alehouses. The aptly named King's Head, linked by a disused sanctuary passage to its towering cousin, is one of only five such establishments to survive the centuries. Today it offers an atmospheric real-ale venue the walls of which are graced by old photographs – and guns.

Traditional sandwiches provide the main sustenance, bolstered by a popular German import: Bockwurst sausages are served in a baguette with a variety of relishes. Children are not allowed in the three public rooms, which include a poolroom, but there is a pleasant patio/beer garden to the rear. The three hand-pulled bitter beers – Tetley, Stones and Worthington – are finely presented, alongside hand-pulled Bass mild, Tennent and Carling Black Label lagers, Autumn Gold and Dry Blackthorn ciders and draught Guinness. The inn has three letting bedrooms.

Opening times are Monday to Saturday 11 am to 11 pm. Sunday hours are 12 noon to 10.30 pm.

Telephone: 01482 899314.

How to get there: The inn is on the corner of Souttergate and Magdalen Lane in the centre of Hedon, east of Hull along the A1033.

Parking: Park in the inn car park to the rear. Alternative parking is available round the town green, north of the church.

Length of the walk: 1¾ miles. OS Map Landranger series 107 (inn GR 188287).

A surprisingly rural excursion around the precincts of the splendid old church and along the route of a dismantled railway line.

The Walk
From the front of the inn go forward towards the church and swing right, crossing to the left-hand side of the town green. Go left along Ivy Lane. Just beyond the end of the cemetery, turn right through a

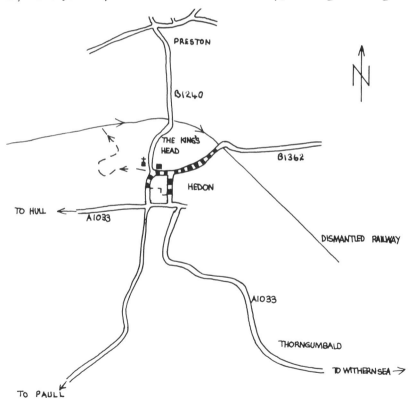

swing gate marked Elsie Gate and swing right close to the hedge. In the corner, swing right and keep beckside, then swing left, crossing the beck on a footbridge. Turn right and go left, crossing the beck again on a wide concrete farm bridge.

Follow the footpath left across a field, and turn right along the old railway line. Continue to Preston Road. Cross and continue along the old railway line (with a fishing lake to the left). Turn right at the B1362 and walk along the roadside footpath for about 500 yards to the B1240 junction.

Turn left on Baxtergate, passing the Shakespeare (another heritage inn), and turn right as if visiting the Hedon Catholic church. Turn right again, walking on at the back of the Shakespeare and go left on George Street. Turn right on Market Place, back to the inn.

Other local attractions: St Augustine's church (its size and opulence reflect the former prosperity of Hedon). Also, 2½ miles south-west, is the little-known hamlet of Paull. This tiny place has also declined. Warships were built here and it was once a strategic defensive position guarding the Humber and the port of Hull. Fort Paull has been restored as a visitor attraction, exhibits including waxworks, an underground hospital and a network of labyrinths, passages and bomb stores, antique guns and other weapons, military vehicles and tableaux. There is an entry fee and it is open April until October. Telephone: 01482 893339.

Fort Paull

Beverley
The Monk's Walk

5

In the glorious shadow of Beverley Minster and with uninterrupted views of its tower from the rear beer garden, the Monk's Walk is a tempting retreat from the bustle of the nearby markets. A historic 14th and 15th century den for real ale connoisseurs, its narrow interior is graced by a well-sooted hearth, a period ghost and a bijou restaurant

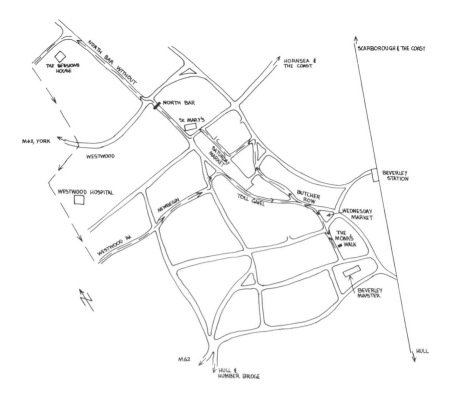

with a wizened timber roof that displays the ancient technique of pegging. The inn, as with many other buildings in the fascinating town of Beverley, has an interesting past. See the 1671 datestone in the passage. Friars are said to have passed this way escorting coffins en route from the Minster to the nearby burial grounds.

The tally of CAMRA-recommended ales, lagers, ciders and stouts is impressive – dither over the choice of hand-pulled Castle Eden, Flowers, Marston's Pedigree, Old Speckled Hen and Black Sheep, with Heineken, Heineken Export and Stella Artois lagers, Scrumpy Jack and Red Rock ciders, and draught Guinness and Murphy's stouts. The seasonally adapted menu embraces a wide selection of fish, poultry, meat and vegetarian dishes and includes deep-fried brie, melon with fresh fruit in Gran Marnier, grilled tuna, lemon sole, monkfish in white wine, spicy chicken, chateaubriand, liver and onions, vegetarian stir fry and aubergine and pepper omelette. Children are welcome in the restaurant.

The inn is open Monday to Sunday 12 noon to 11 pm (10.30 pm on Sunday).

Telephone: 01482 862710.

How to get there: The inn is on Highgate, south-east of the town centre near to the Minster.

Parking: The inn has a rear car park. Frontage on-street parking is limited, but there are a number of free public car parks nearby.

Length of the walk: 2 miles. OS Map Landranger series 107 (inn GR 037394).

An architectural and historical adventure exploring one of the finest townscapes in England.

The Walk
Turn right from the inn along Highgate, cross Lord Roberts Road, using the pedestrian crossing, and go straight forward into Wednesday Market (pedestrianised). Walk on and, where the route divides, swing right on Walkergate and continue without deviation at the bend for a further 50 yards. Turn left along Dog and Duck Lane and turn right along Ladygate towards St Mary's church. Turn left at Hengate and turn right at North Bar Within. Although we have only covered a few hundred yards, such is the wealth of interest along the route – did you spy the stone carving of a hare in St Mary's (this bunny inspired Lewis Carroll to create the White Rabbit)? – that you may be in need of refreshment. Beverley is renowned for its ice-cream and Burgesses has its parlour near the North Bar.

Continue under the gateway and proceed over the crossroads along North Bar Without and New Road for about a ¼ mile, crossing to the alternative footway in front of the Sessions House. Go left on Norfolk Street and walk on to a kissing gate at the end. Go through and turn left on to the famous Westwood, an attractive common rivalled only by Harrogate's Stray. Keeping to the perimeter, continue through a second gate (racecourse to the right) and go left through a grey, galvanised gate, turning right on a track to York Road. Cross, turn right for 5 yards and fork left on a metalled footway, ascending and passing the Westwood Hospital to your left.

Swing left to Westwood Road and turn left, crossing the junction and proceeding along Newbegin to join Lairgate. Turn left and opposite No 14, turn right into Saturday Market. Turn right again, continue along Toll Gavel and bear left, retracing your steps back to the inn.

Other local attractions: A jewel among market towns, Beverley has, in addition to its Gothic minster and its equally fine church of St Mary's, numerous other attractions – a market cross and two market places

23

(Saturday Market and Wednesday Market), an ancient gateway (North Bar), numerous quality shops, cafés and restaurants, the Museum of Army Transport, a racecourse (14 flat meetings every year) and Highgate Corner, a highly recommended tearoom on the corner near the inn (try the scones).

Foston on the Wolds
The Plough

6

Originally an alehouse, the whitewashed Plough is a friendly and adaptable family run inn whose attractions extend to bed and breakfast accommodation, a Caravan Club site and take away fish and chips served on Wednesdays and Fridays. Blessed by open fires in winter and corn dollies, this spacious inn serves a popular and an extensive range of home-made bar meals, the standard choices including steak and kidney pie, rack of lamb, steaks, haddock, plaice, salmon and trout. The daily specials board lists, for example, lasagne, chicken Kiev, beef curry, halibut mornay, lemon sole and sticky toffee pudding. Sunday lunches are a speciality. Children are welcome for meals. The inn also has a rear picnic area. The hand-pulled bitters are John Smith's and Black Sheep plus a revolving guest beer. Lagers are Foster's and Stella. Woodpecker cider and draught Guinness are the alternatives.

The inn is open Wednesday to Sunday 12 noon to 3 pm (not open Monday and Tuesday lunchtimes). Evening hours Monday to Sunday are 7 pm to 11 pm.

Telephone: 01262 488303.

25

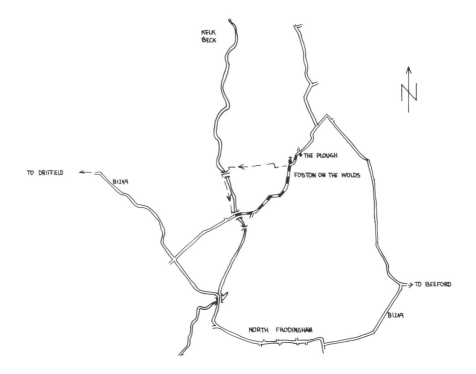

How to get there: The inn is in the village of Foston on the Wolds, off the B1249 about 6 miles south-east of Driffield.

Parking: Park in the inn car park.

Length of the walk: 2½ miles. OS Map Landranger series 107 (inn GR 102559).

A leisurely ramble over fields, along the banks of the Kelk Beck and through the pretty village, which is almost as long as its name.

The Walk
Turn left from the inn and go left round the bend. Just beyond the church, go right and follow a public footpath sign. Lift the sneck and open a green door (it gets curiouser and curiouser) and go left through what appears to be a private garden. This really is a public right of way – the ancient route of farmworkers to the fields. Weave left to a gate, go through and keep straight forward over a meadow. At the green

26

gate, go right (the OS map edition of 1986 is in error here and the route has been diverted as in my directions) for 200 yards and go left at the marker post.

Continue on a track between two fields and go left alongside the Kelk Beck to the bridge. Go right over the bridge and then left along the bank to the bridge. Go left along the road (footway after 300 yards), walking through the village back to the inn.

Other local attractions: A must for the children – Cruckley Animal Farm south of the village (50 varieties of farm animals including rare species, seasonal demonstrations, daily milking and a nature trail).

Harpham
The St Quintin Arms

The St Quintin Arms, named after a dynastic family whose generations rest in the nearby church, is the type of inn that makes the émigré Englishman pine for home. Sensitively adapted and cared for with a pride that glows like church silver, this is a heritage inn, a hideaway venue to be enjoyed and savoured.

Open fires, oak panelling, delph racks and a captivating collection of original paintings and prints set the scene for leisured dining. Flair and imagination shine through in a menu, adapted to the seasons, which features clam fries, omelettes, a medley of steak dishes, lasagne verde, chicken à la king (with mushrooms and peppers in a cream sauce), rainbow trout, haddock and wheat and walnut casserole. The daily specials board may include cheese and broccoli soup, chicken breast in a tarragon sauce, chicken and ham pie, kings and queens (prawns and scallops) en brochette, wrapped in bacon with a mousseline sauce, tuna and pasta bake, and halibut mornay. Sunday lunches are very popular. Children are welcome for meals. In addition to a good wine cellar, the inn offers hand-pulled John Smith's and Courage Directors bitters, Foster's lager, Woodpecker cider and three stouts – Guinness, Beamish and Murphy's. The inn has four letting bedrooms (one with a four-poster bed) and a delightful rear patio and beer garden.

Opening hours are Monday to Saturday (not open Monday and Tuesday lunchtimes) 12 noon to 3 pm and 7 pm to 11 pm. Sunday hours are 12 noon to 3 pm and 7 pm to 11 pm.

Telephone: 01262 490329.

How to get there: The inn is ¾ mile south of the A166 Driffield to Bridlington road, near Burton Agnes.

Parking: Park in the inn car park.

Length of the walk: 2½ miles. OS Map Landranger series 101 (inn GR 092617).

This short stroll has everything . . . a church, an ancient well with a legend to boot (the little drummer boy – ask the landlord), hedgerows, the pellucid waters of the Kelk Beck and, at the end of it, Yorkshire puds and two veg.

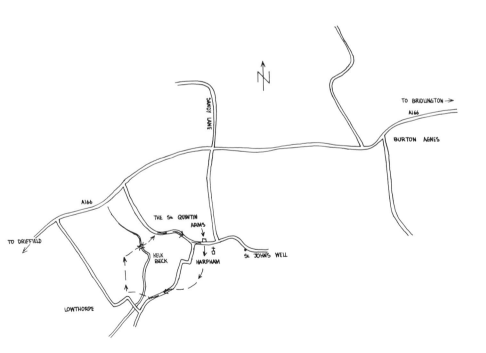

The Walk

Go through a kissing gate opposite the inn, following a public footpath sign. Continue forward hedgeside to a second kissing gate, go through and walk straight on with the lawn tennis court to the left. Cross a stile and go right, following the direction marker, and find a bridge near the edge of a pond. Go right over the bridge and follow a public footpath sign across a field, steering left to the road (if in crop, go round).

Bear left along the quiet road for 400 yards and turn right, following the public footpath sign through a gate, and walk on, crossing a bridge over Kelk Beck. Go left for 10 yards and cross a ditch on a footbridge, then turn right ditchside. Swing left in the field corner and go straight forward, following a marker post. Cross an old gate (makeshift stile), follow a barbed wire fence down alongside the young plantation and, at the field corner (no sign), go right hedgeside to a green gate. Go through and turn right to a second green gate. Go through this and continue hedgeside.

About 20 yards before the field corner, turn right over a stile, following the direction marker, and go left to a track. Turn right on the track, walking on in the direction of a wood, and recross the Kelk Beck on a bridge. Continue straight forward to the left of the corrugated barn, cross the stile by the farm gate and continue to the road. Turn right, back to the inn.

Other local attractions: Harpham is said to have been the birthplace in AD 640 of St John of Beverley. Dedicated to him, the local church has some of the finest brasses and monuments in the county. See also the local wells, particularly St John's Well east of the village. It is reputed to cure all ills.

Burton Pidsea
8 The Nancy

Built in 1851 the Nancy is a charming little inn, snuggling under the eaves of St Peter's church. With a workaday bar and a restful lounge exposing its ancestry in a preserved forge and anvil, the inn is ideal for walkers and offers wholesome bar meals and real ales.

The menu includes cottage pie, fillet steak, chicken Kiev, goujons of plaice, omelettes and a vegetarian dish of the day. Sunday lunches are a speciality. Children are welcome for meals. Burtonwood beer is available on tap, together with Carling, Stella Artois and Carlsberg lagers, draught Guinness and Autumn Gold cider.

Opening times are Monday to Saturday 11 am to 11 pm. Sunday hours are 12 noon to 10.30 pm.

Telephone: 01964 670330.

How to get there: The inn is in the village of Burton Pidsea, 10 miles east of Hull.

Parking: Park in the inn car park.

Length of the walk: 3 miles. OS Map Landranger series 107 (inn GR 252312).

A leisurely amble along a cart track and a country lane.

The Walk

Turn left from the inn, passing the church of St Peter, and turn left again on Carr Road. After 200 yards go right along a signposted public bridleway. Swing left and right on the track and follow telegraph poles down for about ¾ mile, going left at the top of a young plantation. Continue on a track, cross a culverted ditch and swing right and left, walking on hedgeside.

At the end of the hedge, go left towards Elmtree Farm on a track. Continue along the metalled road into Burton Pidsea. Turn right, following the public footpath sign going between a gate post and a wall pillar, and walk on keeping right fenceside. Go through a gap in a wall and turn left by Dashwood House, back to the inn.

Other local attractions: At Halsham, 4 miles south-east, a beautiful temple of stone – a mausoleum built for Sir William Constable in 1792.

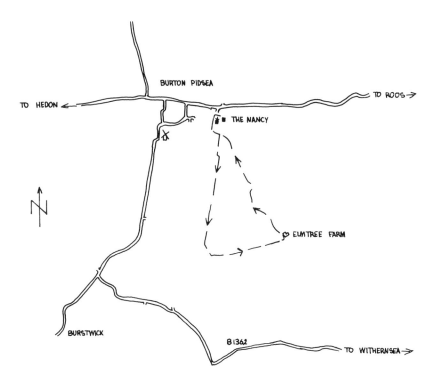

Blacktoft

9

The Hope and Anchor

A licensed lighthouse with its barrels below the water line, the Hope and Anchor shares its riverside berth with buoys and beacons. At an ancient Ouse ferry point, the inn is remote but immensely cheery, offering a comfortable bar adorned with photographs of old river craft and a homely dining-room with views of the flow. From the levee you can see the Blacktoft Sands RSPB Nature Reserve across the stream. On fine days you can make the most of the riverside seating and the little beer garden.

A family-run freehouse, the inn serves value-for-money bar meals. There is soup of the day, 7″ Yorkshire puddings with onion gravy, breaded mushrooms filled with soft cheese and garlic, steaks, steak and kidney pie, tagliatelle carbonara, breaded chicken breast stuffed with prawns and lobster, and beef or chicken pieces in oyster sauce. Sunday lunches are a speciality. Children are welcome for meals. The liquid fare is hand-pulled John Smith's, Old Mill, Boddington and Theakston bitters, Kronenbourg and Foster's lagers, Dry Blackthorn cider and draught Guinness.

Opening times are Monday and Tuesday 4 pm to 11 pm;

33

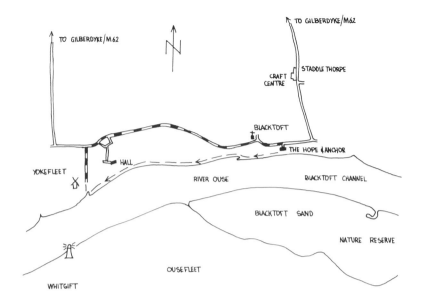

Wednesday to Sunday 12 noon to 11 pm (10.30 pm on Sundays).
Telephone: 01430 440441.

How to get there: The inn is in the village of Blacktoft on the north
bank of the Ouse, south of Gilberdyke. It is best approached by
leaving the M62 at junction 38 and going south-west through Newport
and Gilberdyke.

Parking: Park in the inn car park.

Length of the walk: 3 miles. OS Map Landranger series 106 (inn
GR 845242).

A short riverbank and country lane amble returning through Blacktoft village.

The Walk
Turn right from the back of the pub along the river embankment and
walk on to Blacktoft jetty. Continue following the bank, cross a creek
and go immediately left over two stiles to regain the bank path. Walk
on under power lines to Yokefleet creek, noticing the old windmill
and across the river the lighthouse between Ousefleet and Whitgift.
Turn right along the road into Yokefleet and turn right again at the
junction, following the quiet tree-lined road to Blacktoft. You will

pass along the way two lodges, West Lodge and East Lodge. Examine the inscriptions on the gate pillars – 'CORUNA MEA CHRISTUS'.

In Blacktoft, see the pretty cottages and visit the interesting church of St Clement's. A number of drowned sailors are buried in the churchyard.

Other local attractions: On the access road from Gilberdyke, South Farm Craft Gallery (pottery, doll's houses, general crafts and a courtyard tearoom and restaurant). Blacktoft Sands Reserve is a must for ornithologists, although, since the demise of the Blacktoft Ferry, it is a 20-mile road journey from here, via Goole. It has spectacular views of reedbed birds, offers observation hides, wheelchair access and free parking (admission charge), and is open every day except Tuesdays.

⓾ Driffield
The Bell

Built in 1742 before the canal brought prosperity to Driffield, this inn is a Yorkshire institution presenting an unassuming face to Market Place. As you enter, tip your cap to a bell that has speeded many a stagecoach on its way and prepare to be surprised.

The Bell provides a high standard of accommodation and facilities, at real value-for-money prices. There are 14 en suite bedrooms, a snooker room, a swimming-pool and a gym equipped with a sauna, a solarium, a Jacuzzi and something called a float tank. I am told by NASA boffins that this is something they developed to simulate weightlessness for astronauts. It has been adapted by the leisure industry to enable stoics, nonchalant of being enclosed in a light-sealed, warm, brine-filled coffin, to achieve a state of nirvana. Outside, within 800 yards, the inn has a 20-acre garden.

The Bell has been considerably extended over the years, absorbing what was once a thoroughfare to the rear together with the old town hall. Hung with original etchings, engravings and paintings on a Yorkshire theme, it offers the biggest oak-panelled bar in Yorkshire for buffet lunches and bar meals, a dining-room and a sumptuously furnished restaurant. Doorstep queues speak volumes for the buffet

36

luncheon menu, which features, for example, home-made soup, roast leg of pork carved from the trolley, roast duckling in orange sauce, chicken chasseur, lamb in rosemary, braised steak, leek and potato bake and rhubarb sponge and custard. The dinner bell (rung at 7 pm) heralds restaurant specialities such as smoked mackerel with garlic, royal game soup, coquilles St Jacques (scallops in a cheese sauce served in a shell), chicken à la crème, pork fillet, entrecôte marchand du vin (a sirloin steak cooked in a sauce of red wine, onions, bayleaf, peppers and thyme) and Dover sole. In addition to a selection of over 200 whiskies, the inn serves hand-pulled Younger Scotch, Younger No. 3, Directors and John Smith's bitters (the tally of beers is constantly changing), Carlsberg lager, Strongbow cider and draught Guinness.

Opening times are Monday to Wednesday and Friday to Saturday 10.30 am to 2.30 pm and 6 pm to 11 pm. Thursday (market day) hours are 10.30 am to 10.30 pm. Sunday hours are 12 noon to 2.30 pm and 7 pm to 10.30 pm.

Telephone: 01377 256661.

How to get there: The inn is on Market Place in the centre of the market town of Driffield.

Parking: Park in the rear car park. Free parking is also available close by.

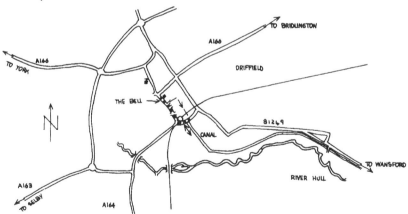

Length of the walk: 1 mile. OS Map Landranger series 107 (inn GR 024577).

A walk to a delightful picnic spot on the Driffield Canal.

The Walk

Turn left from the inn on Market Place, following the sign to the railway station, and go left after 150 yards under an archway (easily missed) on Providence Place. Turn right beckside and just past the Women's Royal Voluntary Service building, go left over a footbridge, continuing on Bridge Lane. Turn right opposite the Mariner's Arms. On the bend, swing left by the Albion Street sign and walk down the cul-de-sac towards the pedestrian bridge over the railway line.

Cross the bridge and go right to River Head. Pass the old crane and go left opposite the Blue Bell Inn and walk past the converted former warehouses and a canalside picnic area. This area was once busy with barges and the highly distinctive Humber Keels. The canal, which opened in 1722, allowed grain and other agricultural products to be shipped direct to Hull. Now only waterfowl disturb its surface.

Retrace your steps back to River Head. Go left at the Blue Bell Inn and swing right over the level crossing by the railway station. Turn right on Middle Street South, back to the inn.

Other local attractions: Fosse Hill Jet Ski Centre at Brandesburton, 10 miles to the south-east – jet ski and go-kart hire, adventure playground, bar and shop.

⑪ Patrington
The Hildyard Arms

This recently modernised roadside inn has long been prominent in local affairs, as the record of Sir George Head's visit in 1835 shows:

> The corn market in Holderness is held once a week in the Hildyard Arms at Patrington, whither the cornfactors, three of whom entirely divide the country, arrive at four o'clock; consequently, during the winter, all the business is transacted by candlelight . . . The staircase of the inn all the time is a thoroughfare, whereon the farmers continually stump up and down in their heavy boots, with a sample-bag in one hand, and not unfrequently, a glass of hot gin and water in the other . . . The company chiefly drank hot toddy, and smoked tobacco . . . a wealthy man actually brought with him a couple of friends to participate in the recreation of pipe and spittoon.

A bright and cheery inn, the Hildyard Arms has adapted to the times, providing accommodation, bar meals and summer barbecues, real ale, live entertainment and a family room equipped with a pool table. As well as traditional fare such as grilled chicken, steaks and scampi, the inn serves Chinese meals Cantonese style. The house ales are hand-

39

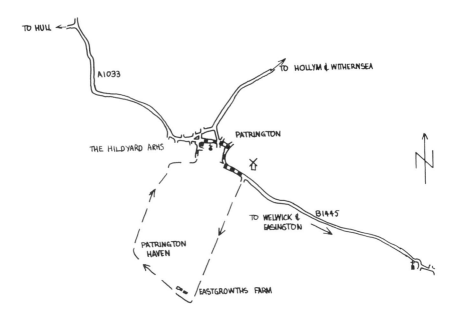

pulled Tetley and Bass. The alternative brews are Carlsberg and Labatt's lagers, Woodpecker cider and draught Beamish stout.

The Hildyard Arms is open daily from 12 noon (11am on Saturdays) to 11 pm (10.30 pm on Sundays).

Telephone: 01964 630478.

How to get there: The inn is in the centre of Patrington on the B1445 just south of the A1033 Hull to Withernsea road.

Parking: Park in the rear car park or in the street.

Length of the walk: 3 miles. OS Map Landranger series 107 (inn GR 314226).

A gentle Patrington/Patrington Haven circuit along quiet footways and farm tracks. The walk is blessed all the way by the soaring presence of St Patrick's church.

The Walk

Turn right from the inn past St Patrick's church. A mariners' beacon for centuries, this is one of the finest parish churches in England. A visit to Patrington is not complete without proper exploration and a

40

climb up the spiral staircase (the keys are available).

Using the footway, continue to the bend and go right on the signposted Welwick Road. Go round the next bend, and opposite the stub of the old windmill go right along the signposted public bridleway. Continue for about 1 mile and go right on a marked bridleway opposite Eastgrowths Farm. Continue along a track and a metalled access road into Patrington Haven. Turn right, using the footway, and walk on into Patrington. Swing around the bend in the direction of St Patrick's and turn left along Greenshaw Lane, back to the inn.

Other local attractions: The seaside resort of Withernsea 4 miles north-east along the A1033 (beach, amusements, cafés and a lighthouse museum).

⑫ Holmpton
The George and Dragon

The village of Holmpton suffers badly from coastal erosion but the recent investment at the smart but externally unassuming George and Dragon is good for 100 years yet. So you can plan ahead at your leisure, perhaps savouring the prospect of elegant dining, Italian style. The artistic bricklayer who transformed the George and Dragon must have cake decoration in his blood. His swirling bonding, creating arches, arcades and a pair of sumptuously crafted fireplaces could hardly be bettered with a piping nozzle. The overall effect of the restaurant is enhanced by soft pastel furnishings and the finest tableware.

Bar meals, served in the more prosaic stone-flagged games area, include roast beef, spare ribs, chicken breast Milanese, goujons of sole, seafood pancake and spaghetti carbonara. The à la carte restaurant fare features home-made soup, fresh lobster, suprême of chicken Dijon, rainbow trout and shrimp soufflé, escalope of pork normande, tournedos rossini and a wide range of Italian dishes such as petto di pollo alla crema (chicken in a white wine, parsley, mushrooms and fresh cream sauce) and bistecca alla Portoghese (sirloin steak in a wine and tomato sauce with garlic, onions, green peppers and mushrooms).

Children are welcome for meals. The bar-top line-up is hand-pulled John Smith's and Tetley bitters and Fosters lager, draught Beamish and Guinness stouts and Woodpecker cider. The inn has a beer garden to the rear.

Opening times are Monday to Friday 12 noon to 3 pm and 6 pm to 11 pm; Saturdays 11 am to 11 pm; Sunday hours are 12 noon to 10.30 pm.

Telephone: 01964 630478.

How to get there: The inn fronts the road opposite the church in the village of Holmpton, south-east of Withernsea.

Parking: Park on the gravelled car park opposite the inn.

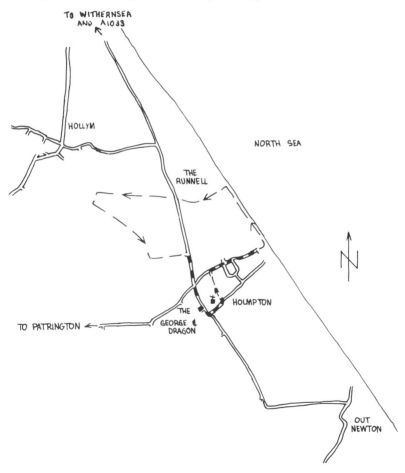

Length of the walk: 3 miles. OS Map Landranger series 107 (inn GR 366234).

A coast and fields ramble. The path I describe may not exist for much longer, such is the rate of coastal erosion in these parts. On a recent previous visit, the Claff Farm barn was still intact. Look at it now!

The Walk

Turn right from the inn along the road for 100 yards and go left. Pass the church and go next left along a signposted bridlepath. Turn right at the road and walk on to the cliff top. The doomed Claff Farm is immediately to the right. Turn left and continue along the gradually descending cliffs, passing a pill-box and a brick structure. Go left at the dyke known as The Runnell and walk on to the road.

Cross the road and go straight forward, following a public footpath sign along the edge of a garden. Cross a footbridge over a ditch and walk on, following a line of telegraph poles to an access road. Go left for 200 yards and swing sharp left. Swing right, going through a gate and over a ditch, and after 400 yards swing sharp left again to the road, going right, back to Holmpton and the inn.

Other local attractions: Fishing is good from the beach.

13 Bishop Wilton
The Fleece

Their eminences, the Archbishops of York, would steal away to their summer palace in a village that is still the prettiest in the Yorkshire Wolds. Set in a luscious amphitheatre of green hills with long distance views of the Pennines and the westerly escarpment of the Cleveland Hills, Bishop Wilton sits serenely beside its beck, the tranquillity of the place with its fascinating archaeology, ancient church and inviting old inn being rarely matched anywhere in the county. Owned by Lord Halifax, the Fleece is a comfortable and uniquely furnished outpost of nearby Garrowby Hall, open fires, rustic bygones, sporting prints and original works of art creating the perfect atmosphere for relaxed dining. Its stylish, ever changing menu typically includes Stilton and onion soup, fresh jumbo haddock, sea bass, braised beef and ale pie, and braised lamb shank. The house ales are John Smith's, Tetley's, Black Sheep and revolving guest ales.

The inn has a pleasant beer garden and offers overnight accommodation (two doubles and two twins).

Opening times Monday to Saturday are 12 noon to 3 pm and 6.30 pm to 11 pm (10.30 pm on Sundays).

Telephone: 01759 368251.

How to get there: Bishop Wilton is 13 miles east of York. The inn is signposted off the A616 York to Driffield road, a few hundred yards up the ascent of Garrowby Hill. Turn right on the lane for ⅓ mile.

45

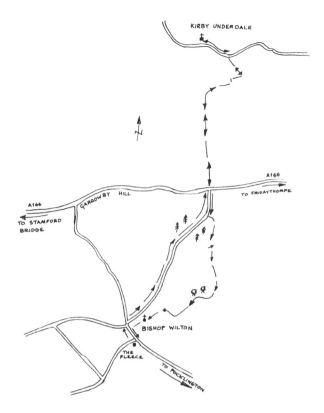

Parking: Park in the inn car park or on Main Street.

Length of the walk: 6 miles. OS Map Landranger series 106 (inn GR 798552).

This exhilarating walk has compass-spinning views of the Vale of York, the Cleveland Hills and the Pennines. With an ecclesiastical and pastoral theme it takes in a network of field and hill paths, the site of the Archbishop's Palace and two historic churches.

The Walk
Turn left from the inn along the lane for 200 yards and turn right up Worsendale Road. Pass the playing fields to the left and continue uphill. The next field on the right is the moated six-acre site of the Archbishop's Palace. The complex once included a large hall, a library, dormitories, kitchens, a dispensary and fish-ponds. The palace was abandoned by the disgraced Archbishop Neville in 1400.

46

Walk up the steep hill (motor traffic is very infrequent) to the summit and the junction with the A166.

Cross the A166 and take the track immediately opposite continuing straight forward and dropping down to the right of a narrow wood. Go through a gate and continue forward and down to a second gate and go through the side gate, descending another 100 yards on a track to a third gate.

Turn right off the track, crossing a stile and follow a footpath sign, veering left over a field to the corner. Near the corner, go left through a fourth gate and follow the narrow stream down for 50 yards to a fifth gate and turn right uphill following the hedge upwards to a sixth gate. Go through left for a few strides to a stile and cross left into a sloping field, descending to a stile in the corner. Cross and turn left on the lane, dropping down to Kirby Underdale and the delightful church of All Saints. To the left of the porch path is the relocated base of a cross that once marked a boundary line of the Archbishop's Palace. Inside, set into a wall, is a Roman relief of Mercury. Tucked away, round the back of the church, are several memorials to the Wood family (Earls and Countesses of Halifax).

Retrace your steps back to the A166 and cross, going down Worsendale Road for 100 yards.

Turn left through the edge of the wood following the footpath sign and swing right following the ridge path for about 400 yards. Turn left at the back of Flat Top House at the wood edge, walking up to a gate.

Go through and turn right keeping to the edge of the wood. Near the wood corner veer left to a stile and cross, dropping down left and climbing up to the top of the crest. Keep forward towards the seat. Near the seat, is one fan's tribute to the *Lord of the Rings*. Walk round right dropping down and rising again in an arc right and go left at the wood edge following the fence down to a stile. Cross left and turn right over a descending field heading towards Bishop Wilton. Steer left through a clump of hawthorn bushes to a stile and cross, dropping down left to a gate.

Go through and turn right on a track, dropping down left. Pass the cottage and turn right on the road uphill for a few yards towards the school. Go left past the cottages to the church. St Edith's was exquisitely restored by Sir Tatton Sykes in 1859. Its tiled floor is based on an original in the Vatican.

Keep going straight forward and turn left back to the inn.

Other local attractions: Just a couple of miles east of Kirby Underdale on the road to Thixendale at Fotherdale Farm, is the studio and gallery of wildlife artist Robert Fuller.

14 Burton Agnes
The Blue Bell

Once part of the Burton Agnes Hall estate, this 200-year-old former coaching inn has blossomed under the care of a chef/landlord whose hearty bar meals are fit for any lord. Served in the cosy dining-room or in the open-fired rustic bar the choice includes home-made steak and kidney pie, roast duckling in orange sauce, various steak dishes, omelettes, chicken curry, fillet of fresh Scarborough cod and haddock, a selection of vegetarian meals and seasonal sweets such as bread-and-butter pudding and black cherry pie. Sunday lunches are a speciality. Children are welcome for meals. Convenient for coast-bound holidaymakers, the inn has overnight parking for five caravans (breakfast available). There is a small games room and a pleasant patio/beer garden to the rear.

The house ales are hand-pulled John Smith's, with Labatt's lager, Dry Blackthorn cider and draught Guinness.

Opening times are Monday to Saturday 11am to 2.30pm and 7pm to 11pm. Sunday hours are 12 noon to 3pm and 7pm to 10.30pm.

Telephone: 01262 490379.

How to get there: The inn fronts the A166 road in the village of Burton Agnes, 5 miles south-west of Bridlington.

Parking: Park in the inn car park.

Length of the walk: 3½ miles. OS Map Landranger series 101 (inn GR 103629).

A fields and quiet lanes circular route with opportunities to explore the architectural and historical treasures of Burton Agnes and Harpham.

The Walk

Go straight forward from the inn along the road to Rudston (Burton Agnes Hall to the right). About 100 yards after the Burton Agnes sign go left, following a signposted path, and continue down alongside a fence. Keep straight forward at the corner of the cricket field and cross a big field using the well-defined path, walking up to a gap in the hedge near to the twin power-cable poles. Veer right on the footpath, heading for a group of three trees and, maintaining the same general direction, continue on a path across the next field to a stile. Cross and keep the same bearing, walking across a field to the corner. Go through a gap by the gatepost and turn left on Sandy Lane. Continue to the road. Cross and keep going straight forward towards Harpham.

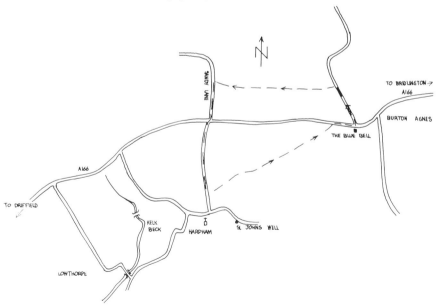

This village will fascinate walkers who are interested in English history and a detour to visit it is well worthwhile. The ancient church has some of the finest brasses in the county and there are a number of medieval wells in the locality. Turn left at the junction and walk on for about 400 yards to discover the intact St John's Well. Retrace your steps to the chapel conversion to continue the walk.

About 100 yards before the junction (just beyond the chapel conversion) go left, following a public footpath sign over two stiles. Go left again, following a direction marker, and head for a lone tree, cross a stile under the tree and go straight forward, following a distinctive footpath. Swing right, following a direction marker hedgeside, and after 200 yards go left over a stile and turn immediately right, following a ditch for 250 yards. Swing left across a field on the well-defined footpath to the field corner, cross a ditch on a planked footbridge and cross a stile, going slightly left and cutting off the field corner, to another stile. Cross and steer right to the road. Cross a stile and go right, back to the inn.

Other local attractions: Burton Agnes Hall (an outstanding Elizabethan house open to the public – collections of furniture and paintings. Garden includes a maze).

15 Allerthorpe
The Plough Inn

A comely inn built some 250 years ago, the Plough was much frequented by bomber crews during the Second World War. Today she entertains a quieter set, providing nutritious, good-value bar and restaurant fare in attractive surroundings. An inn of intimate little bars and crannies, decorated cottage style, the Plough serves a medley of home-made dishes – Yorkshire puddings and onion gravy, chargrilled chicken, gammon and steaks, spare ribs, beef and mushroom pot pie and daily specials such as green pea and ham soup, breast of chicken Madeira and seafood thermidor. Children have their own menu. Sunday lunch is popular (booking advisable). The inn has a well-equipped poolroom and picnic tables for the summer months.

Ales are Theakston, Tetley and Black Sheep with Carling and Stella lagers and draught Guinness.

Opening times are Monday to Saturday 12 noon to 3 pm and 5.30 pm to 11 pm. Sunday hours are 12 noon to 3 pm and 7 pm to 10.30 pm.

Telephone: 01759 302349.

How to get there: The inn is in the village of Allerthorpe, south-west of Pocklington and ½ mile from the A1079.

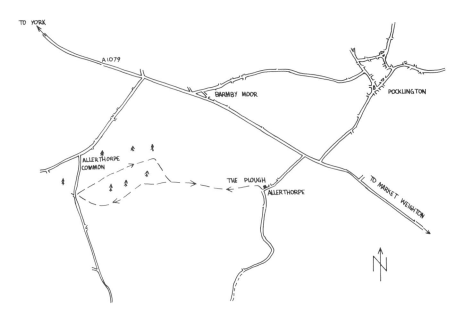

Parking: Park in the rear car park or in front of the inn.

Length of the walk: 4 miles. OS Map Landranger series 106 (inn GR 784474).

A sylvan circuit of Allerthorpe Common. Parts of the afforested area are now being restored to heathland. Enjoy woodland scents and cedar sighs.

The Walk

Turn right from the inn and right again along the lane to the side of the inn. Swing left after 50 yards, following a marked public bridleway. Pass the farm and continue along a hedgeside, crossing a beck and bearing left towards woodland. Keep straight on into the wood and walk on into a conifer plantation. Go left at the Forestry Commission sign and follow the well-defined path nearly to the road. Just before the gate, turn sharp right on to a forestry access road.

Continue for about a mile and follow the track to the right, swinging left to the Forestry Commission sign. Go forward, retracing your steps back to the inn.

Other local attractions: Burnby Hall Gardens (one of the best water lily displays in Europe) in Pocklington.

52

Newton upon Derwent
The Half Moon

The Half Moon has surrendered its thatch, but it concedes little else to 20th century licencedom. A 19th century village institution brimful of character, part pub, part sweet shop and social centre, it offers robust ales, simple but hearty meals and a warm welcome to strangers.

Toast yourself by the fire in the single L-shaped bar in winter, or enjoy the grassed seating area to the rear of the pub in warmer weather, and select from a bar menu which includes special home-made chilli and mince, steak pie, grilled steaks, giant Yorkshire puddings, omelettes and Sunday special roasts. Children are welcome for meals. Ales include John Smith's and Bombardier, with Kronenbourg and Foster's lagers, Woodpecker and Dry Blackthorn ciders and draught Guinness.

Opening times are 12 noon to 3 pm and 6 pm (7 pm on Sundays) to 11 pm (10.30 pm on Sundays).

Telephone: 01904 607452.

How to get there: The inn is in the village of Newton upon Derwent,

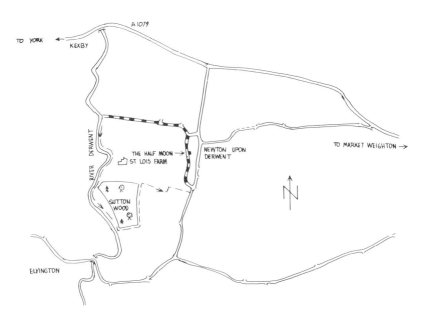

1 mile due south of Wilberfoss and the A1079 York to Market Weighton road.

Parking: The inn has small car parking areas to the front and side. Alternative parking on the street.

Length of the walk: 4 miles. OS Map Landranger series 106 (inn GR 721495).

A watermeadows ramble along the banks of the Derwent, returning through woodland which is bright with flowers in spring.

The Walk
Turn right from the inn along the street and, at the bend, fork left along a road signposted as a cul-de-sac. Swing left and walk on for about a mile to a stile. Cross and go right for 100 yards to the river bank.
Follow the Derwent for about 1½ miles, and 500 yards past the Yorkshire Water intake and compound on the far bank go left away from the river to the corner of Sutton Wood (wild daffodils and bluebells in April). Cross a stile and a planked bridge and keep to the edge of the wood, swinging left and right to a gate and stile. Cross and

go immediately left, following the waymarker on the telegraph pole stay, walking alongside the edge of the wood to the north-east corner. At the corner keep going forward 100 yards to the St Lois Farm access road.

Turn right and swing left and right to the road. Turn left for 100 yards and go left again, following the road signposted 'Newton upon Derwent Village Only'. Swing right back to the inn.

Other local attractions: Yorkshire Air Museum at Elvington, 4 miles south-west (telephone: 01904 608595). Barnes Wallace and Blackburn collections, a flight of vintage warplanes (Halifax, Mosquito, Hawker Hunter, Meteor, Buccaneer), licensed NAAFI and shop. Entrance fee.

⑰ Old Ellerby
The Blue Bell

Other than being as old as the hills and a one-time watering-hole for the famous Hornsea amazon Rose Carr, the humble Blue Bell has a new claim to fame – winner of a recent Pub of the Year award. The inviting interior has open fires in winter, tiled floors (just the job for boots) and three simply furnished rooms, decorated with country knick-knacks. The welcome is warm and cheery and, as no food is available, walkers are invited to bring their own sandwiches. Tea, coffee and biscuits can be provided for pre-booked walking parties.

The house ales are Tetley, Burton and a guest ale, with Carling Black Label lager, Strongbow and Woodpecker ciders and draught Guinness. Children are welcome during daytime opening hours and a play area is provided to the side of the inn. The landlord encourages inspection of a rear pond, a habitat for rare plants.

Opening times are Monday to Friday 7 pm to 10.30 pm (closed midday). Saturday 12 noon to 4.30 pm and 7 pm to 11 pm. Sunday 12 noon to 3 pm and 7 pm to 10.30 pm.

Telephone: 01964 562364.

How to get there: The inn is in the village of Old Ellerby north-east of Hull and east of the A165 Hull to Bridlington road.

Parking: Park in the inn car park.

Length of the walk: 4¼ miles. OS Map Landranger series 107 (inn GR 168375).

Fields, woodland edges and lanes make up this rural circuit, blessed with a myriad of bluebells in spring. So near to the city . . . but so far away. Who says walking is a popular pastime? I never saw a soul!

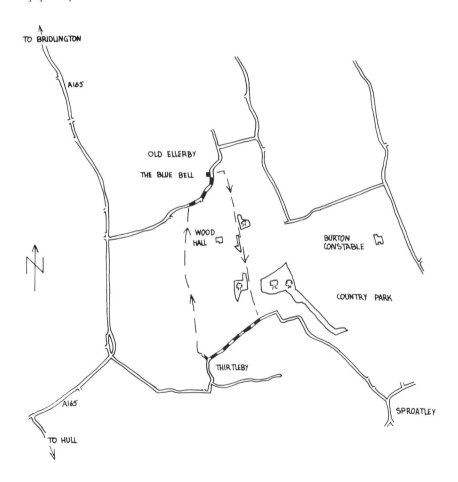

The Walk

Leave the front door of the inn and cross the road, going forward, following a public footpath sign and a line of telegraph poles over a field. At the field edge, turn right, following the direction marker hedgeside. Continue on a clearly defined footpath heading for a wood. Follow the direction markers and go down the right-hand side of the wood. At the wood corner, turn right and swing left alongside a narrow belt of trees. At the top end of the third wood, pass through a gap in the hedge, go right for a few paces, then left hedgeside, dropping down to the lane.

Turn right along the lane, pass the greyhound kennels and continue for about ½ mile. Go right on the bend, following the signposts to Mount View Farm and Stillmeadow. Continue past the hen runs (the metalled road peters out, giving way to a farm track), swing left to a public bridleway sign and go forward on a broad path, passing to the side of a wood. Walk on to the road and turn right, back to the inn.

Other local attractions: Burton Constable Hall – about 4 miles by road, south-east. This is a splendid Elizabethan house with works by Chippendale, Adams and James Wyatt. The extensive Capability Brown parkland displays include collections of agricultural machinery, horsedrawn carriages and 18th century scientific apparatus.

⓲ Barmston
The Black Bull

A 1930-vintage holidaymakers' inn catering for families, the Black Bull can be found in the village of Barmston, a survivor of centuries of erosion which has claimed over 2 miles of land since Roman times. The accommodation describes a segmented circle, giving the three public rooms and their bars curvaceous lines. The comfortable lounge bar, dressed in red velvet, overlooks the well-equipped children's play area and a caravan park to the rear. There is also a taproom, a poolroom and a beer garden.

The menu features home-made soup, large Yorkshire puddings filled with braised steak and mixed vegetables, lasagne, Barnsley chop, a choice of griddled steaks and fresh haddock. Sunday lunches are a speciality but must be booked ahead. Children are welcome for meals. The house brews are hand-pulled Tetley and John Smith's, and Kronenbourg and Carlsberg lagers, Autumn Gold cider and draught Guinness. The Black Bull looks over a most delectable pond.

Opening times Monday to Sunday are 12 noon to 3 pm and 7 pm to 11 pm.

Telephone: 01757 288849.

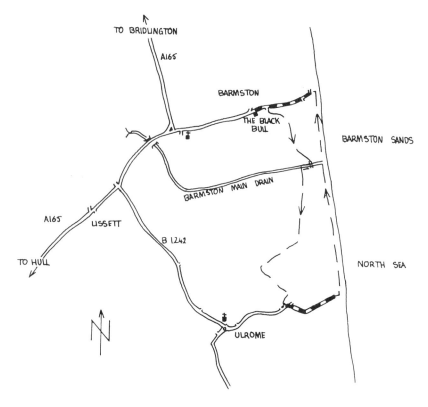

How to get there: The inn is in the seaside village of Barmston south of Bridlington, off the A165.

Parking: Park in front of the inn.

Length of the walk: 4¼ miles. OS Map Landranger series 107 (inn GR 163593).

A bracing fields and cliffs walk. The clutch of strategically placed pill-boxes makes you ponder the carnage that would have been Barmston Beach.

The Walk

Turn right from the inn on the roadside footpath and continue for about 300 yards. Turn right, following the public footpath sign, cross a stile and pick up a track going left. Continue on the track to Barmston Drain. Go right, crossing the drain on the outfall bridge, and turn right, following the drain away from the sea for about 200 yards. Just beyond the pill-box on the little knoll to your left, turn left and follow a well-defined footpath for about ¾ mile, then turn right on a metalled road.

Turn left towards the hamlet of East End and at the bend go right, following the public footpath sign over a stile. Go left through a caravan site and turn left at the road. Go round two bends and continue towards the sea. Keep straight forward at the next bend and turn left along the low cliff-top path. Continue past Barmston Drain to Barmston and turn left along the road, back into the village and the inn.

Other local attractions: Magical little church of All Saints (tomb chest of 1446), Jacobean manor house of the Boyntons and, south-west of the inn (reached by public footpath), a calvary of tortured trunks – one man's monument to the curse of Dutch elm disease.

⑲ Huggate
The Wolds Inn

A hilltop inn, externally distinguished by its century-old sign and a pair of monumental entrance bollards impressed with the hieroglyphics of the licensed trade, the Wolds Inn has served the travelling public for over 400 years. Recently refurbished to a high standard, it offers facilities for both the booted and the clean shod. Choose the informality of the public bar or the elegance of the oak-panelled restaurant, enjoy the long-distance views and ruminate on the temptation of a 20-oz steak, knowing that this establishment has a reputation for 'Yorkshire portions'. Try a wedge of home-made steak pie, a loin of pork cooked in cider, half a roast duckling, a serving of marinated venison, a lemon sole or a round of excellent sandwiches and select your brew from hand-pulled Tetley and Timothy Taylor's Landlord and a revolving guest beer, Carlsberg lager, Gaymers Olde English cider and draught Guinness. Children are welcome for meals. Traditional Sunday lunches are popular and it is advisable to book ahead. The inn has four en suite letting rooms and a pleasant summertime seating/play area to the rear.

Opening times (closed Monday lunchtimes) are daily 12 noon to 2 pm (2.30 pm on Sundays); evenings 6.30 pm to 11 pm (Sundays 7 pm to 10.30 pm). Telephone: 01377 288217.

How to get there: The inn is on a minor road south of the A166 York to Driffield road and 5 miles south-east of the Garrowby Hill summit.

Parking: Park in the inn car park.

Length of the walk: 4½ miles. OS Map Landranger series 106 (inn GR 883551).

A roller-coaster ramble along parts of the Wolds Way, enjoying the characteristic landscape of rounded chalk hills and dry valleys. Some climbing is necessary.

The Walk
Turn right from the inn along the road and turn right again following the sign 'Village Only'. Walk on past the church and drop down to a junction of farm access roads, taking the right fork, signposted 'Wolds

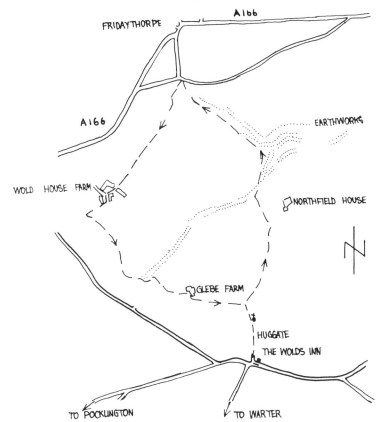

Way'. Continue uphill, following the public bridleway sign and pass the 'Northfield Farm' sign. Proceed for a further 200 yards and go left hedgeside, following a public bridleway sign.

At the end of the field, cross a stile (vestiges of earthworks here) and go right for 20 yards along the crest, before steering diagonally left downhill towards a copse in the valley bottom. Go left in the bottom over a stile, following the 'Wolds Way' sign.

Swing right at the end of the valley uphill and walk on to a gate, going sharp left following a public footpath sign. Cross the next stile, keep fenceside, and in the corner turn left for 50 yards, then turn right to follow a farm track between two fields. Continue to Wold House Farm. Cross the farmyard and go left to the farmhouse, noticing a bronze tribute to farmhand David Midgley who was the foreman hereabouts for over 30 years. Turn right along the access road for 300 yards and go left, following a hedge line. Swing right and drop down into a valley, going straight forward to find a stile in the bottom. Cross and go left, walking uphill to the crest.

Continue left along the crest for 400 yards and turn right over a stile next to a blue-barred gate. Follow the fence down to a farm access road and turn left. After 150 yards veer right on a farm perimeter path and merge with the access road, continuing to the junction. Turn right, back to Huggate and the inn.

Other local attractions: Just a couple of miles east of Kirby Underdale on the road to Thixendale at Fotherdale Farm, is the studio and gallery of wildlife artist Robert Fuller.

20

Seaton Ross
The Black Horse

Serve the ale in teacups and the front parlour scene would be complete. I have been in inviting and relaxing pubs before, but never have I had everything but slippers! I suppose it's the cushions that do it. One for each elbow, they almost outnumber the collection of pot cats and dogs that inhabit the fireplace. Floral printed curtains, luxurious soft seating and a traditional menu which includes leek and potato pie, grilled steaks, chicken cordon bleu, plaice with prawns, ham and beef salads and jam roly-poly make for cosy and memorable visits.

The bar-top offerings are hand-pulled John Smith's and Tetley bitters (together with a guest beer), Carlsberg and Foster's lagers, Woodpecker and Scrumpy Jack ciders and draught Guinness. Children are welcome for meals and are especially catered for in the conservatory, which is reserved for non-smokers. The inn also has a taproom/games room with a pool table. There is a farmyard area to the rear where the displays are interactive – children may experience the ponies, goats, cows, turkeys and guinea-fowl at close quarters.

The inn is not open at lunchtimes except on Sundays – 12 noon to 3 pm. Evening hours are Monday to Saturday 7 pm to 11 pm and Sunday 7 pm to 10.30 pm.

Telephone: 01759 318481.

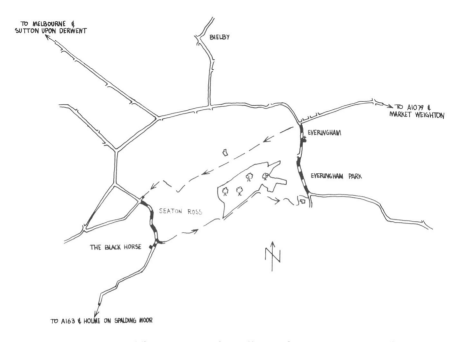

How to get there: The inn is in the village of Seaton Ross north-west of Holme on Spalding Moor (access from the A163).

Parking: Park in the inn car park.

Length of the walk: 4½ miles. OS Map Landranger series 106 (inn GR 782408).

A cross-fields route to the delightful village of Everingham with a return through porker country.

The Walk

Turn left from the inn and go right down Mains Lane. Turn left opposite the cottage, going through a gap in the conifer hedge. Follow the public footpath sign over a planked bridge and steer diagonally right over a large field (route indistinct), heading for the right of a large plantation. Go right for the field corner and look out for a rickety bridge over a ditch. Cross and go right for 50 yards and look out for a yellow marker directing you across the apex of a field. Cross the field and follow the dyke up, keeping to the edge of the plantation.

Walk on for ⅓ mile and turn right over a footbridge, continuing on a track. Follow the track down and swing left by the farm and its pond, going right alongside the farm buildings and left to the road. Walk on into Everingham.

Continue through the village and just before the T-junction turn left, following a public footpath sign over a stile. Follow the yellow direction markers. At the bottom of the field, go right for 10 yards and turn left crossing the bottom of a field between a fence and hedge. Continue hedgeside, cross a planked footbridge and keep forward, heading in the direction of a wood. Continue down the farmer-defined track (pig farm), cross a field and go left over a footbridge, following the direction markers. Keep hedgeside for one field and turn right on a track for ¼ mile. Turn left on a track to the road, and turn left, back to the inn.

Other local attractions: Don't fail to see the amazingly large and opulent Chapel of the Virgin and St Everilda at nearby Everingham. This mini St Peter's was built to joyously signal the end of Catholic persecution after the Act of Emancipation in 1829. (Take the A614 north-east from Holme-on-Spalding Moor and take the first turn left going through the hamlet of Harswell. Proceed for a mile into Everingham. The edifice can be seen through the trees on the right.)

North Newbald
The Tiger

21

Eyeing the neighbouring Gnu Inn, the Tiger looks out on the Wolds and on an extensive village green, circled with period cottages. Built around 1820, the unspoilt inn offers a warm welcome and a variety of dining options. Bar meals are served in the comfortable twin bars. Upstairs is a large dining-room for more formal occasions. Choices range from traditional Sunday lunches to vegetarian dishes. Home-made steak and kidney pie, grilled steaks and Whitby haddock are popular. Daily specials include fresh venison, supplied from a farm across the green. The watering-hole dispenses hand-pulled John Smith's, Timothy Taylor's Landlord and Black Sheep, with Foster's lager and draught Guinness.

Opening times are 11am to 11pm daily, Sundays 12 noon to 10.30pm.

Telephone: 01430 827759.

How to get there: The inn is in the village of North Newbald, off the A1034 north-west of Hull.

Parking: Park in the inn car park.

Length of the walk: 4½ miles. OS Map Landranger series 106 (inn GR 913368).

An up and down walk with lovely views. I used to feel like this when we went to grandma's and bounced on her feather bed. The Wolds are equally good fun . . . and you won't get clipped round t'lug!

The Walk

Turn left from the inn and go left on Eastgate. (Venison is for sale at Hall Farm.) Go left along East Wold and follow the footpath uphill. At the road, go left and right, following the signposted public footpath up Dot Hill. At the summit, follow the line of telegraph poles straight

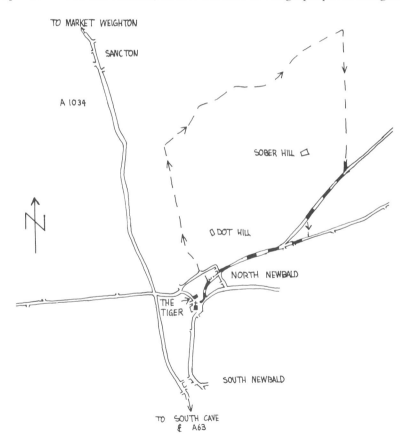

ahead and walk on downhill to the back of Syke House Farm.

Turn right, following the direction marker, and walk on a curving path in the bottom for about 1 mile, to a stile. Cross and go left towards a wood and a gate. Cross a second stile and continue woodside, heading for power lines. Walk under these, swing right and go left hedgeside heading for twin telegraph poles. Turn right on a public bridleway and continue to the road. There is a tombstone to the old cartographers' craft down this path. Made redundant by satellite mapping techniques, triangulation pillar S6295 lies abandoned to the weeds.

Turn right at the road for 250 yards (Flower Hill Farm is along this road to the left) and turn left, following the Wolds Way sign down a track to another road. Turn right along this quiet lane, back into North Newbald.

Other local attractions: About 5 miles south-east of North Newbald (take the minor road to Little Weighton and turn right to Rowley) is the fascinating settlement of Rowley consisting of no more than a hotel and a church – St Peter's. Suffering religious persecution in 1638, most of the local inhabitants upped-sticks and left with their vicar – the Reverend Ezekiel Rogers – for America. A commemorative stained glass window was installed in 1994 which tells the story of the quest for religious freedom. See also the illuminating entries by American ancestors in the visiting book.

Commemorative stained glass in St Peter's church, Rowley

22 Roos
The Roos Arms

Farming implements grace the frontage of this appealing little inn, the popular resort of locals and holidaymakers from nearby Withernsea. Dating from 1784, the Roos Arms has a back bar with an open fire, a relaxing snug, a dining-room and a rear patio.

A good reputation soon spreads amongst the bucket and spade fraternity and it is advisable to arrive early in the busy summer months in order to enjoy the varied bar menu, supplemented by daily specials. The standard listings are home-made soup, deep-fried brie, baked pasta, waldorf au gratin, calamari, seafood puff (puff pastry case filled with prawns, mussels, scallops and mushrooms in a sauce of white wine and grapes), crêpes, Dover sole, lemon chicken en croûte, Durham lamb (in a Cumberland sauce of orange, lemon and redcurrants) and tournedos rossini. Specials include beef in Guinness, steak pie, oriental stir-fry beef and roast of the day. Sunday lunches are a speciality and children are welcome for meals. The liquid offerings are hand-pulled Tetley and Worthington bitters (plus occasional guest beers), Foster's, Carlsberg and Kronenbourg lagers, Dry Blackthorn cider and draught Guinness.

Opening times are Monday to Friday 12 noon to 3pm and 6pm

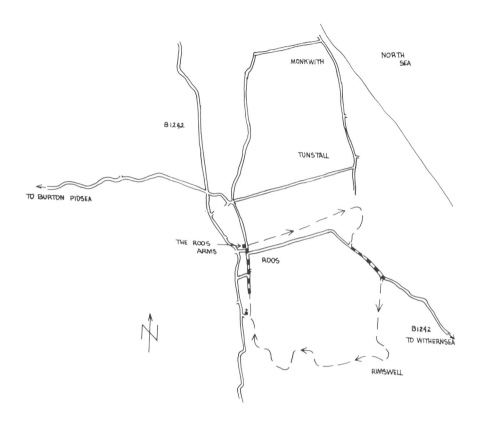

(5 pm on Thursdays and Fridays) to 11 pm. Saturday and Sunday 12 noon to 11 pm (10.30 pm on Sunday).
Telephone: 01964 670353.

How to get there: The inn is on the main street in the centre of the village of Roos, 4 miles north-west of Withernsea on the B1242.

Parking: Park in the car park to the rear.

Length of the walk: 4½ miles. OS Map Landranger series 107 (inn GR 290306).

A mainly hedgesides, lanes and drain banks ramble. Largely undisturbed, the Roos drain habitat supports breeding tawny owls. Contrary to popular belief, they can be seen during the day.

The Walk

Leave the front entrance, cross the road and go straight forward, following a signposted public footpath between a hedge and back garden fences. Continue hedgeside, swing left for 50 yards and go right, following the direction marker, then walk on ditchside. Cross a footbridge, keep ditchside, go left for 10 yards and continue, alongside the ditch to the road. Turn right. At the junction go left (no footway and at times the road can be busy) and walk on the grass verge for a little under ½ mile.

Turn right along the road signposted to Rimswell (quiet byway), go left and right round two bends, walking on for 150 yards to the next bend. Turn right, following a public footpath sign along the concreted access to Carr Farm. Keep straight on, passing farm buildings to the right, continue at the side of the tennis court and follow the footpath down to a small copse. Steer right, following the marker post, keeping left of the drain bank. Follow the drain round, going right then left. Cross a planked bridge and keep drainside, carrying on to a T-junction of drains (owls hereabouts).

Turn left and follow the loop of the drain for about ⅓ mile and find a footbridge, going right over the bridge and left fieldside. Follow the drain round and where it divides, go right in the direction of the church, joining a cart track. Swing left towards the road for 100 yards and swing right and left at the edge of a field, walking up to the right of the church. Go left at the back of the sewage farm and then right.

Go left over a stile into the church grounds and go through the kissing gate, continuing on a back road past houses and cottages into Roos. At the junction, keep straight forward, back to the inn.

Other local attractions: The seaside resort of Withernsea, south-east along the B1242 (beach, amusements, cafés and a lighthouse museum).

73

㉓ Skidby
The Half Moon

The 300-year-old village inn at Skidby is a shrine to a dish – one that is to walkers what Kendal mint cake is to explorers. The prize-winning Yorkshire puddings here are hatched from loaf tins and consume 70,000 eggs and 7,000 lbs of flour each year. As the Half Moon's ode to 'Yorkie' has it, 'Not only have natives from all parts of the British Isles devoured them but visitors from at least 27 countries have sampled the delights of our speciality Man-Sized Yorkshire Puddings served thus:

With Onion Gravy

With Vegetarian Curry

With Minced Beef and Mushroom

With Roast Beef and Onion Gravy
(our butcher hangs finest topsides of bullock beef
. . . definitely not cut with a laser)

With Toad in the Hole

With Lamb in the Hole
(suck the bones clean for best effect)'

The alternative dishes are steak and kidney pie, roast chicken, scampi, curry, chilli and a selection of burgers. Children are welcome for meals.

The house ales are hand-pulled Marston's Pedigree and John Smith's bitters, and Chestnut mild. Foster's, Kronenbourg and Carlton LA lagers and Beamish stout are also on tap. In addition to the attractive split-level lounge, hung with old pictures, the inn has a characterful taproom, retaining elm tables and a tiled floor. A popular outside attraction is the extensive beer garden equipped with slides and a climbing contraption that would test the SAS.

Opening times are 11 am to 11 pm (Sunday to 10.30 pm). Telephone: 01482 843403.

How to get there: The inn is in the village of Skidby between Hull and Beverley, to the west of the A164.

Parking: Park in the inn car park.

Length of the walk: 4½ miles. OS Map Landranger series 106 (inn GR 019337).

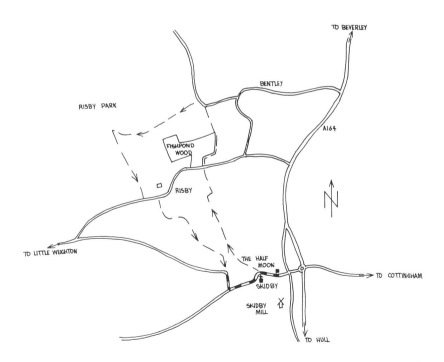

A gently undulating hedgerows ramble, spiced with long-distance views of Beverley Minster.

The Walk

Turn right from the inn along Main Street, passing the village stores and Quarry Farm. Walk on to the bend and go right, along Church Rise, continuing for 100 yards to join a marked footpath. Continue forward on a well-defined route and go right to a gate and a stile. Cross and walk on in a narrow hollow between two fields and swing left on to the edge of a field. Maintaining the same direction, continue fieldside (Beverley Minster comes into view), swing right for 200 yards and go left towards the road and a wood.

Cross the road, turn left for 5 yards and turn right over a stile, following a marked footpath at the edge of a wood. Swing right and go left, keeping woodside to the corner. Keep going forward, passing a telegraph pole and continuing to a stile and a road. Walk down the road for 100 yards and go left over a stile, following a marked public footpath hedgeside.

Continue hedgeside towards a wood (Risby Estate) and when past it, swing left and right and drop down to a stile. Cross and continue on a track, dropping down and then ascending to join a farm access. Go left on the trackway to a road. Turn left for 300 yards towards a red-bricked house and turn right over a stile, following a marked public footpath hedgeside. Turn left in the field corner, walk on for 250 yards and turn right over a stile, continuing on a tussocky path between two fields. Swing left under the power lines and then right to Little Weighton Road.

Turn left, walk on to the bend and swing left. Opposite Chapel Close, fork right by St Michael's church, continue at the side of the village green and proceed down Main Street, back to the inn.

Other local attractions: Skidby Windmill (built in 1827), 5 minutes' walk south. In full working order, the mill is open Tuesday to Saturday 10.30 am to 4 pm and on Sundays 1 pm to 4.30 pm (small admission charge).

24 South Cave
The Fox and Coney

Built in 1739, this former coaching inn has returned to its roots, providing eight bedrooms for overnight guests and a large, characterful public bar, sporting an open hearth, rustic prints and a grandfather clock. The bar menu is cosmopolitan and extensive and includes a range of flame-grilled steaks, steak and kidney pie, roasts (Sundays only), chicken Kiev, breaded turkey, ham and mushroom tagliatelle, chicken tikka masala, cheese and broccoli flan and jumbo cod. The daily specials board regularly lists five alternative dishes such as beef in ale pie and ham and mushroom flan. Children are welcome for meals.

The cellar is equally well stocked, the choices including hand-pulled Tetley, John Smith's and Timothy Taylor's Landlord, with Foster's, Stella and Carlsberg lagers, Autumn Gold and Scrumpy Jack ciders and draught Guinness.

Opening times are Monday to Friday 11.30 am to 2.30 pm and 4.30 pm to 11 pm. Saturday 11.30 am to 11 pm. Sunday 12 noon to 10.30 pm. Telephone: 01430 422275.

How to get there: The inn is in the village of South Cave just north of the A1034/A63 junction, north-west of Hull.

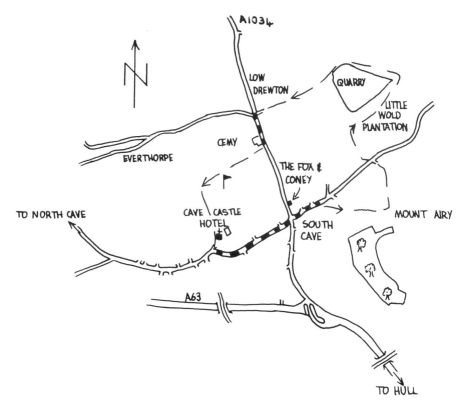

Parking: Park in the inn car park.

Length of the walk: 4½ miles. OS Map Landranger series 106 (inn GR 923314).

A breezy Wolds Way orbit of chalk and tees – hills, woodland and a fairway.

The Walk

Turn left from the inn and go left on Beverley Road. Just before the bend, turn right, following a signposted footpath going left up Airy Hill, keeping left of a copse halfway up the slope. Walk on to the hill-top road and turn left, following the Wolds Way sign downhill to the road. Turn left for 100 yards and turn right over a stile, following the Wolds Way sign uphill to the edge of Little Wold Plantation. Turn right into the edge of the wood and walk on past the chalk quarry to the left, continuing to the road. Turn left and then swing left to the quarry entrance and continue downhill to the road.

Turn left along the A1034, using the footway for 400 yards, and just beyond the cemetery chapel, turn right, following a public footpath sign over a stile. Follow the line of yellow arrow markers affixed to the line of trees on the Cave Castle Hotel golf course and go left at the track towards Cave Castle. Cross a stile by a gate, turn right at the back of All Saints church and go left by the entrance to the hotel, walking on the roadside footway into the centre of South Cave. Turn left at the junction, back to the inn.

Other local attractions: Cave Castle – a yellow brick pile, built in 1804, with angle turrets and battlements – All Saints church (American visitors on the heritage trail delight at discovering the inscriptions WW 1700 and RW 1701 carved into the pillars near the pulpit – the graffiti of George Washington's forebears!) and the 1796 Market Hall near the inn.

25 Millington
The Gate Inn

The Gate Inn is the cosiest place around. A 16th century building with a pantiled roof that matches the contours, it has two bars, log-flamed in winter, and an adjoining games room. There is a hikers' version of the Sistine Chapel ceiling. Raise up thine eyes and plan your route, using a map pickled by decades of bar smoke.

Cribbage boards and wind-tanned complexions set the scene for relaxed eating, the girding menu including speciality home-made steak pie, steaks and chicken dishes, gammon and eggs and delicious fruit sponges. Children are welcome for meals. Barside, the line-up is hand-pulled Tetley, John Smith's and Black Sheep bitters, Castlemaine and Lowenbrau lagers, Gaymers Olde English cider and draught Guinness.

The inn is not open at lunchtimes during the week, but the sneck is off Saturday and Sunday 12 noon to 3 pm. The evening hours are from 7 pm to 11 pm.

Bed and breakfast accommodation is available.

Telephone: 01759 302045.

How to get there: The inn is in the small village of Millington on a minor road, 3 miles north-east of the market town of Pocklington. It can be reached from the A166 or the B1246.

Parking: Park in the inn car park.

Length of the walk: 5 miles. OS Map Landranger series 106 (inn GR 832517).

Elgar, who was uniquely inspired by the English countryside, would have set this Wolds walk to music. The route is very steep in places, with compensating views.

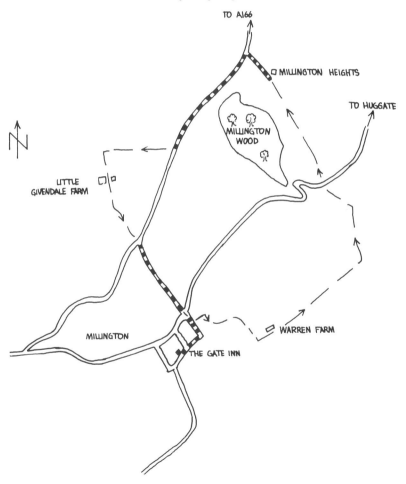

The Walk

Turn left from the inn past Town Farm, swing left round the bend and follow the footpath signposted 'Minster Way'. Fork right downhill on a track. Go through a gate, swing right to a second gate, go through and keep forward to a stile. Cross and steer to the left of the deep hollow, climbing steeply. Join a track and go right and continue ascending. Swing left to a stile, cross and keep going straight forward, crossing two further stiles, and walk on to join a track just below the crest. Turn left, following the Wolds Way sign. Pass the farm and go left, following the Wolds Way and Minster Way signs along a hedgeline. From this vantage you almost have an aerial view of Millington Wood and the course of the old Roman road on the skyline to the left.

Drop down and in the field corner go left, following the fenceline. In the next field corner cross a stile and go right, following a direction marker. Swing left, arcing round a fence for 100 yards, then go right, following the direction marker and dropping down to the bottom of the hill. Go left along the fenceline, cross a stile and a planked footbridge over the stream and continue to the road.

Cross the road and follow a signposted public bridleway (old Roman road) over a stile, ascending to a gate. Go through, swing right by the fence, walk on to a gate, go through, following a public bridleway sign on a track passing to the left of Millington Heights, and continue to the road. Go left (quiet road) for about ¾ mile and turn right, following a public bridleway sign through a gate, dropping down hedgeside to a track.

Turn left to Little Givendale Farm, go straight forward between farm buildings and veer left on a track, continuing to the road. Cross the junction and continue on the road to the next junction. Cross into Millington and swing right, back to the inn.

Other local attractions: Burnby Hall Gardens (one of the best water lily displays in Europe) in Pocklington.

26 Lund
The Wellington Inn

Captured in the viewfinder is the very spirit of village England – an ancient green and cross, a church and a venerable old pub. Britain in Bloom award-winning Lund must be one of the prettiest villages in Yorkshire.

There has been a pub on this site since the 12th century and the pantiled Wellington, although it has considerable modern charms (including a suite of settees that rival water-beds for comfort), retains an air of immutability, expressed in open fireplaces and wainscoting. The atmosphere is unhurried and relaxing. Nod by the hearth and choose from a standard bar snacks menu which includes ranges of steak and pasta dishes, steak and ale pie, scampi, chicken Kiev, chicken and broccoli lasagne and roast ham. Daily specials are enterprising and offer such delights as filleted ling baked in yoghurt and lime.

The house draughts are hand-pulled John Smith's, Timothy Taylor's Landlord and Black Sheep with Carling and Stella Artois lagers, Strongbow cider and Guinness and Murphy's stouts. The inn has a dining area/restaurant, a side conservatory/children's room and a rear beer garden.

Opening times Monday to Saturday are 12 noon to 3 pm and

83

6.30 pm (7 pm on Mondays) to 11 pm. No food at all on Mondays or Sunday evenings.
Telephone: 01377 217294.

How to get there: The inn is in the village of Lund off the B1248, 7 miles south-west of Driffield.

Parking: Park in the inn car park to the rear.

Length of the walk: 5½ miles. OS Map Landranger series 106 (inn GR 972482).

A flat fields and quiet lanes tour visiting the three sleepy villages of Lund, Kilnwick and Lockington.

The Walk
Turn left from the inn on The Green. Did you notice the Grade II listed building? It's the telephone box. Continue on Lockington Road and pass Clematis Farm. After 200 yards, go left over a stile, following a signposted public footpath diagonally right (route marked by white marker posts) and aiming for a field corner. Just before the corner, go right over a stile, steer left, cutting off a field corner, and keep left over a ditch, following a marker post. Maintain the generally diagonally left direction (again following white marker posts) and aim to the left of a wood. In the field corner, go right, cutting off the corner of a field and, keeping to the edge of a wood and a field, walk on to the road.

Turn left on the road and near the Moor Farm access, turn right over a stile, following a signposted public footpath along the edge of a paddock. Turn left at the corner of the barn and walk on at the back of the farmyard. Cross a stile, steer left towards another stile, cross, and maintaining the same bearing, cross a field, heading for the corner. Go right at the edge of two fields and swing left to the road.

Cross the road and go up the Kilnwick House Farm access road, following the signs. At the bend, continue ahead over a stile, cross a meadow and a stream on a footbridge and go right, following a direction marker. Follow the stream and direction arrows round for about ⅓ mile and turn right over a footbridge in the direction of the church, following a signpost marked 'Minster Way'. Go through a gate and, at the road, swing right and go left past the church to the road. At the junction, go forward, walking on the roadside verge (little traffic) and following the signpost to Lockington.

At the junction, turn right for 100 yards and go left on Kilnwick Lane, using the path on the vergeside (again, little traffic) into Lockington. At the next junction, turn left for 300 yards and go right

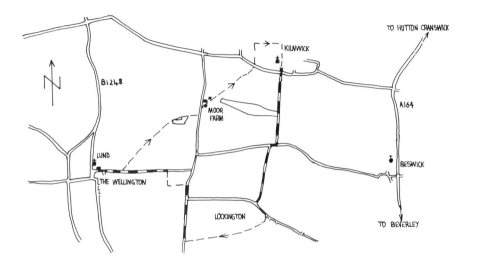

just before the bend, cross a footbridge and continue for 50 yards down Mucky Lane. Go right, following a public footpath sign, going through a gate and aiming left to a second gate. Go through, keep left ditchside, cross a stile and a planked footbridge over a ditch and continue ditchside to the road. Turn right, using the roadside verge (little traffic) and at the bend go left, following a public footpath sign through a white gate. At the field corner, go right hedgeside to the road. Turn left, using the verge footpath, and walk on, back to Lund and the inn.

Other local attractions: Lund is an extremely attractive village and deserves exploration. Its timeless Englishness provided the setting for a pre-war romantic film, *A Lease of Life*, starring Robert Donat. Visit All Saints church and enjoy the old smithy – imaginatively converted to a bus shelter.

ⓔ Little Weighton
The Black Horse

A mere colt, sired by an 18th century inn sadly demolished in the 1960s, the Black Horse ruminates on a peaceful village scene, hushed by views of distant cornfields and a duckpond. A pleasant seating area/duck assembly point is provided at the side. Enjoy your bar snacks al fresco here in summer.

The inn has a large friendly taproom, kitted out for darts and pool, and a comfortable rear lounge furnished in blue velvet. Evocative village photographs line the walls. The daily bar menu features specials such as pork spare ribs, lemon chicken, and plaice stuffed with prawns and mushrooms, the standard choice including home-made steak pie, chilli con carne, chicken curry, gammon and sirloin steaks and prawn sandwiches. Children are welcome in the lounge for meals and Sunday lunches are available. The liquid fare is hand-pulled Tetley Bitter, Bass and a revolving guest ale, the lager is Carlsberg with Autumn Gold cider and draught Guinness.

Opening hours are Monday to Friday 12 noon to 2.30 pm and 6 pm to 11 pm, Saturday 11 am to 11 pm and Sunday 12 noon to 10.30 pm.

Telephone: 01482 843624.

How to get there: The inn is in the village of Little Weighton north-west of Hull and 3½ miles east of the Skidby roundabout (A164).

Parking: Park in the inn car park.

Length of the walk: 5½ miles. OS Map Landranger series 106 (inn GR 989338).

An undemanding country lanes, bridleways and footpaths amble along a chalky rim of the Wolds.

The Walk

Turn right from the inn, pass the pond and go left on Risby Lane (quiet road) for just over a mile. About 300 yards before the red-bricked house, go right, following a signposted public footpath over a stile, and walk on hedgeside. In the field corner go left for 250 yards and turn right over a stile, continuing over tussocky ground between two

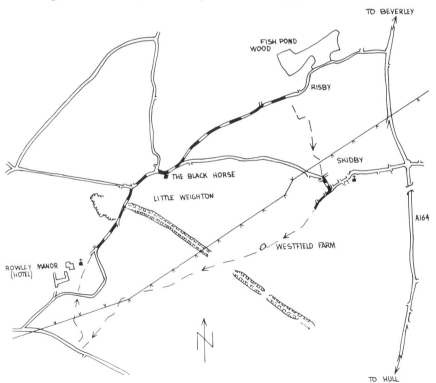

87

fields. Swing left under power lines and then right to the Little Weighton Road.

Go left to the bend and turn right along the cul-de-sac, Riplingham Road. Walk on past the cemetery, continue along a trackway past Westfield Farm and go under the abandoned railway line on a route known as the 'Beverley 20'. Continue hedgeside and walk under power lines, forking left back under the power lines, slightly uphill to a field corner. Go right to the road.

Turn right along the road for 200 yards and turn right again over a stile, following a marked public footpath fieldside. Turn left in the field corner, continue fieldside under power lines and in the corner go right over tussocky ground for 40 yards to a marker post. Go left across the field, aiming for a second marker post midway between two trees. Cross the lane and a stile, following a signposted footpath heading to the right of Rowley Manor.

Cross a stile, steer diagonally right for the field corner and cross two further stiles, going left by the churchyard to a kissing gate and the Rowley Manor access road. Turn right to the entrance gate. Keep straight on at the bend, using the footway at the side of the road, pass the water tower and continue into Little Weighton. Turn right at the junction and go along the Old Village Road, back to the inn.

Other local attractions: Rowley Manor, the one-time rectory to St Peter's Church and now an elegant hotel. The mansion was built at the start of the 18th century and has some noteworthy features inside (particularly the woodwork of the former music room).

Rowley Manor

88

28 Fangfoss
The Carpenter's Arms

Tired of slaking his thirst in the plunging trough, in 1783 the village blacksmith applied for a licence to sell ale and Fangfossians have rejoiced ever since. The modern inn retains all the rustic charms – open fireplaces, time-burnished settles, old photographs and sparkling brasses.

The Carpenter's has three interconnecting rooms and a pleasant beer garden to the side. It serves home-made fare and highly regarded real ale. The traditional standard menu lists ploughman's lunch, chicken and bacon pancakes, grilled gammon, sirloin steak, jumbo sausage and steak pie. The specials board typically offers liver and onions, sweet-and-sour pork, plaice in a mushroom and prawn sauce and Cumberland sausage. There is usually a choice of three sweets – flans, gâteaux and fruit pies in season. Children are welcome for meals and are charged at half the adult rate. The house beers are hand-pulled John Smith's Bitter and Tetley's. The alternatives are Foster's, Carling and Stella lagers, Dry Blackthorn and Scrumpy Jack ciders, and Beamish stout.

Opening hours are Monday to Friday 11.30 am to 3 pm and 5.30 pm to 11 pm. Saturday 11.30 am to 11 pm. Sunday 12 noon to 10.30 pm. Telephone: 01759 368222.

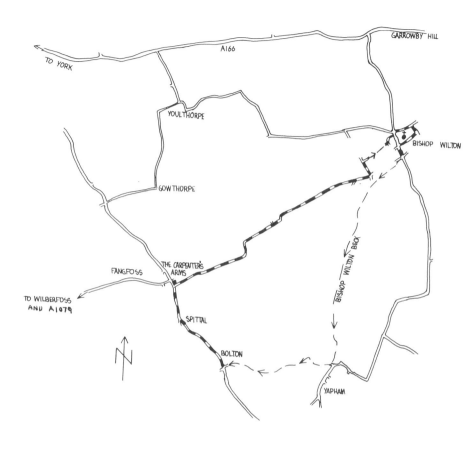

How to get there: The inn is in the village of Fangfoss, 12 miles east of York. It can be accessed either from the A166 or the A1079.

Parking: Park in the inn car park.

Length of the walk: 6 miles. OS Map Landranger series 106 (inn GR 766532).

With voluptuous views of a Wolds escarpment stiffening the sinews, this fairly taxing walk is a real tonic. The halfway stage is the delightful village of Bishop Wilton. Traction can be a problem after heavy rain.

90

The Walk

Turn left from the inn for 15 yards and turn left again along a track, passing a farm to your left. Continue, crossing a beck. Veer right and go left hedgeside, walking on to the bridge over the Salt Beck. Go left for 300 yards and swing right uphill, passing High Belthorpe Farm. Turn left at the side of the farm and then turn right through white gates on to an access road. Continue to the public road. Keep going straight forward at the 'Bolton 3' sign, towards Bishop Wilton, and take the next turn left. Walk on for 400 yards and turn right in the direction of the steeple along a track. Swing left and then right on Vicarage Lane and continue to the road.

Go left and immediately right on the road signposted to Fridaythorpe. Turn next right on the road passing the primary school, and where the road forks, keep to the high path in the centre of the village. Pass St Edith's church to your right. Restored for Sir Tatton Sykes around 1859, the church is beautiful. See the hammer beam roof and its gold leaf decoration and the marbled flooring, which is based on a design from Caesar's palace in Rome.

Continue to the road and turn left past the Fleece inn. Turn next right along South Lane and continue, going straight forward on a track. Swing right to a gate and go left on a track, following the Bishop Wilton Beck down over a series of stiles and ditches to a farm track. Go left through a gate, cross the bridge over the beck and swing right and left. At the field corner go left for 20 yards and turn right through a gate. Cross a field uphill towards the hamlet of Yapham. Go through a gate, cross a farmyard and at the public footpath sign turn right, passing Dormouse Cottage.

Cross the stile on to the edge of a garden (public right of way) and cross a second stile to the edge of a field. The right of way veers off 20° diagonally downhill to the right towards the field corner. (If ploughed over, go left, right and right again.) Turn right at the field corner, along the bottom of the narrow field, and look out for the marker posts (in the hedge bottom). Turn left uphill along the hedgeside to find the route marker. The right of way is indeterminate at this point but you need to steer 20° to your right, aiming for the prominent public footpath sign on the roadside.

Turn left along the road, walk on and turn right at the junction. Using the footway, pass through Bolton and Spittal, back to Fangfoss and the inn.

Other local attractions: St Martin's church (rebuilt in 1849–50 using Norman masonry), and the Rocking Horse Shop (rocking horses, kits, accessories, books and videos) at Manor House Farm.

Hornsea (29)
The Rose and Crown

High-gabled and solidly built in a style contemporary with Noel Coward, this resoundingly English inn is the resort of an endangered species. An immensely friendly place, reeking of beeswax and woodsmoke, it caters for snuff men. Tins of the nasal tonic are available behind the lounge bar, as is a communal pouch of tobacco for the free use of pensioners. A constantly burning gas flame (once as universally common as the spittoon) depresses sales of Swan Vestas. Brasses, tapestries, a collection of teapots in the restaurant and the unlikely upside down figure of a fox prowling the taproom ceiling give the Rose and Crown a distinctive personality. You will always know a good inn by the local company it keeps and seasonal visitors find standing room only at the Rose and Crown.

The inn is famous for its fresh sandwiches and for its home-made pies – meat and potato, chicken, and beef and onion. Scampi, grilled steaks, gammon and oriental dishes are also available and Sunday lunches are a speciality. Children are welcome in the restaurant. The hand-pulled house brew is Marston's Pedigree. The alternative selections are Heineken, Foster's and Stella Artois lagers, Strongbow cider, Guinness and Murphy's.

92

The inn is open daily 11 am to 11 pm (10.30 pm on Sundays). Telephone: 01964 535756.

How to get there: The inn fronts Market Place in the centre of Hornsea.

Parking: Park in the rear car park.

Length of the walk: 6 miles. OS Map Landranger series 107 (inn GR 199476).

Along the Hornsea Rail Trail this walk of contrasts has mere and fields, sea and sand.

The Walk
Turn right from the inn along Market Place and go left on Newbegin. Walk down the length of this road and, where it forks, turn right opposite the library and go down a narrow alleyway. Pass the Hornsea school to your right and keep forward across Football Green, going right, up the embankment of the old railway track at the side of the pedestrian underpass. Turn right along the track and continue to the road. Drop down to the roundabout, go left and right along the street

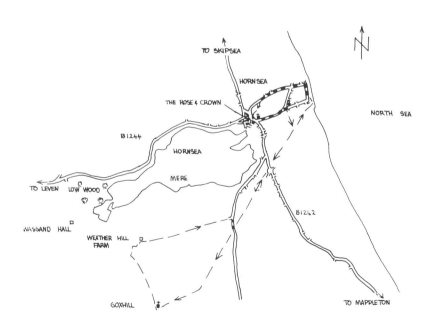

93

running parallel with the embankment and swing left on Edenfield Estate for 70 yards. Go right, following the direction sign for 30 yards, and turn left to regain the line of the railway track. Continue under the bridge and walk on for about ¾ mile.

Nearly opposite the farm, turn right over a culverted drain and swing left drainside. Go right, crossing a drain, and swing left, following the drain in the direction of the hamlet of Goxhill (hidden by trees). Cross a ditch on a footbridge and follow the direction marker, heading across a field (keep to the left of the mid-field copse). Cross a stile and, keeping left of the farm buildings, go through a gate and turn right along the road to Goxhill church. Go left by the church entrance, following the marked public footpath, and steer left of the small pond to find a stile in the field corner. Do not cross the stile, but go left, keeping hedgeside and following the arrow marker. Continue left, following a green path between two fields, and, at the field edge, go left over a stile and turn right hedgeside, following an arrow marker. Follow the field boundary to the left, drainside, cross a stile, maintain the route by the drain to the left of a rookery wood and go right over the culvert, following the direction signs. Turn immediately left through a kissing gate and go right ditchside.

At the next gate steer diagonally right (sign missing) over a meadow at the back of Weather Hill Farm and aim for the field corner. Go through a kissing gate, walk on a short distance through a copse and go left on a track. Turn right along a farm track (views of the mere to the left) and continue to the road. Turn right along the road for 150 yards and go right, dropping down the embankment and going left on the railway track. Continue to the bridge near Football Green and keep on along the track, passing the old railway station (now converted to residential use), to the beach.

Turn left along the foreshore and go left just before the Marine Hotel on Eastgate. Cross the junction and continue along Eastgate. Go left opposite the school into Hall Garth Park and go right on a footpath. Go left on Eastgate, back to the inn.

Other local attractions: Hornsea is a family resort and it offers the usual beachside attractions. Just behind Market Place is the largest freshwater lake in Yorkshire – Hornsea Mere, where fishing, boating, sailing and bird-watching are all popular. Also see the award-winning museum on Newbegin (tableaux of village life and rustic collections) and the justly famous Hornsea Pottery.

30

Holme on Spalding Moor
The Blacksmith Arms

In a mouthwatering livery of black and sherbet, this elegant Georgian inn is like a tempting sweet. Inside you will find the platters clean, as the inn serves no food, but the compensation is in the ale and in the warmest of welcomes. A real locals pub, offering comfort, the charms of a wood-burning stove and facilities for darts, dominoes and pool (the table has a proper slate bed), the Blacksmith Arms serves Burtonwood Bitter with Carling and Stella Artois lagers, Autumn Gold cider and draught Guinness.

The inn is centrally placed for shopping, has a beer garden for children and the doorstep attraction of a bowling green to the rear. Take-away food is available in the town and the shop nearby serves soups, savoury pies and sandwiches.

Opening hours are Monday 5 pm to 11 pm; Tuesday to Saturday 12 noon to 11 pm; Sunday 12 noon to 10.30 pm.

Telephone: 01430 860668.

How to get there: The inn is beside the A163 in the centre of the market town of Holme on Spalding Moor.

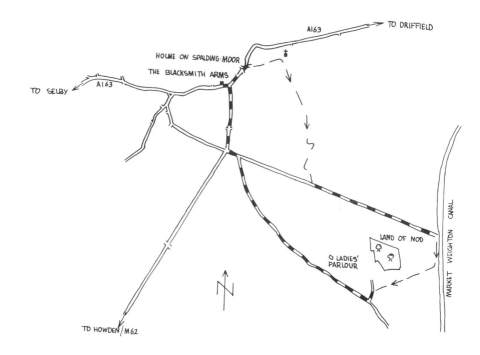

Parking: Park in the inn car park.

Length of the walk: 6 miles. OS Map Landranger series 106 (inn GR 812386).

A trip to the Land of Nod! The route first visits the hilltop church of All Saints before heading off across farmland and down a country lane for the soporific delights of Nodland, a far busier place when it had a pub, the Ship, resort of bargees on the long since desiccated Market Weighton Canal.

The Walk

Turn left from the inn along the main road to the roundabout and go left on the footway alongside the A163, following the direction sign to Bridlington. Cross over the road at the bend opposite the New Inn and take the marked public footpath alongside Stocks Hill Cottages, uphill to the church. Turn right at the top, following the marked footpath down a fenceline to a stile. Cross, go straight forward over

96

a field (route indistinct) and veer left after 250 yards, going downhill towards a ditch. Turn right ditchside and continue following the direction markers to a track.

Turn left for 50 yards and then right, following a signposted footpath alongside a drainage ditch. At the ditch end, go right for 30 yards and then left up the bank, following the direction marker over a field towards the right-hand side of a house. Turn left on Lock Lane and walk on to the Land of Nod. Go right at the end of the lane and follow the public bridleway sign ditchside, walking on to cross a rickety wooden footbridge. Continue ditchside for a further 50 yards and turn sharp right, following successive direction markers fixed to a line of telegraph poles. At the edge of the field, veer left and right and follow the farm track hedgeside, swinging left at the side of farm buildings to Skiff Lane. Turn right and continue for about 1 mile to the junction. Turn left to the A614. Turn right, using the footway, to the roundbout, and go left, back to the inn.

Other local attractions: Don't fail to see the amazingly large and opulent Chapel of the Virgin and St Everilda at nearby Everingham. This mini St Peter's was built to joyously signal the end of Catholic persecution after the Act of Emancipation in 1829. (Take the A614 north-east from Holme-on-Spalding Moor and take the first turn left going through the hamlet of Harswell. Proceed for a mile into Everingham. The edifice can be seen through the trees on the right.)

Easington
31
The Granby

Until the North Sea gasmen came to call, Easington's only visitors were seabirds and hardy caravanners who came in search of the soothing melancholia that is Spurn Point. Opposite the ancient church of All Saints, the Granby sits in sea-cobbled snugness, offering attractive bed and breakfast accommodation (including one four-poster bed), a range of real ales and bar meals, and live entertainment.

In the long, low, comfortable bar, decorated with photographs of the rigs, diners can choose from a range of meals, including cottage pie, chicken and mushroom pie, steak and kidney pie, braised liver and onions, chicken chasseur and roast ham. Sunday lunches are popular and children are welcome for meals. You can sit outside on the pleasant rear patio in the summer months. The liquid offerings include hand-pulled Tetley with Carlsberg lager and draught Guinness.

Opening times are Monday to Friday 12 noon to 3 pm and 6 pm to 11 pm; Saturdays 11 am to 11 pm; Sundays 12 noon to 10.30 pm.

Telephone: 01964 650294.

How to get there: The inn is in the centre of the village of Easington, not far from Spurn Point. Coming south-east from Hull along the A1033, take the right-hand fork (the B1445) in Patrington, signposted to Spurn.

Parking: Park in the inn car park.

Length of the walk: 6 miles. OS Map Landranger series 113 (inn GR 399192).

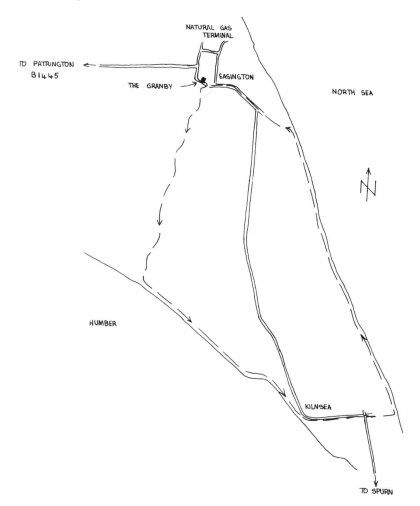

From one side of Yorkshire to the other. An estuary and seashore beachcombing extravaganza. If you take along children with a fetish for unusual stones, you will need to reinforce their pockets.

The Walk
Turn left from the inn, cross the road to the left of the church and walk on to the left of the White Horse inn. Continue on Back Street, swinging right, and go second left on High Street, then right on Humber Side Lane. Continue, following the lane to the riding centre, and keep on until you reach the Humber bank. Turn left along the embankment, continuing for about 1¼ miles to Kilnsea.

Turn left along the road and, at the bend, keep going straight forward to the beach. Turn left at the edge of the caravan park and pass the coastguard station. There is a fascinating Second World War heavy-gun emplacement here. Pass the lagoons to the left (NRA bird hide open to visitors). At the caravan park, go left on the road and keep going straight forward at the bend, into Easington and back to the inn.

Other local attractions: At the back of All Saints church, a remarkable 14th century thatched tithe barn.

32 Market Weighton
The Londesborough Arms Hotel

A handsome 18th century former coaching inn, rescued from dereliction by an award-winning restoration scheme, the Londesborough Arms Hotel is a luxurious roost for the footsore, offering accommodation and a menu to make the toes curl up in excitement. Diners have a choice of either the friendly informality of the bistro, or the silver service opulence of the French gourmet restaurant. In addition, in the summer months, barbecues are organised on the patio to the rear.

The bistro menu, heralded by a full English breakfast, features steak and kidney pie, seafood bake, chicken and vegetable stir-fry and daily specials. The restaurant fare includes starters such as puff pastry with ducks' livers in a port sauce and chicken and hare terrine with truffle and pistachio, followed by poetically described main courses: 'calf's liver quickly fried and set on a savoury pudding base with a chicken and thyme velouté; doriale of chicken forcemeat filled with mushroom, red pimento and ham and served with a chicken consommé; a melody of fresh fish steamed and served with a saffron sauce; and pork royale with a mushroom cream sauce.' And if you will go the whole hog, why not finish with a rum baba: 'a yeast dough

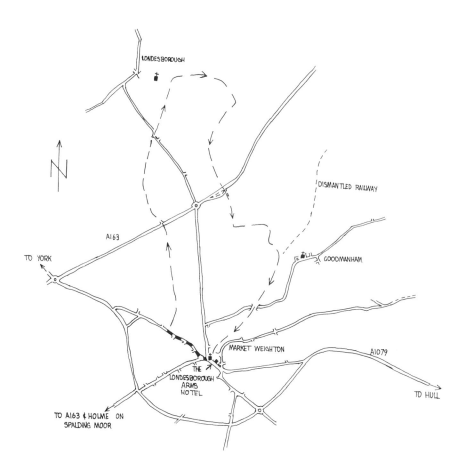

laced with rum and raisin and sealed in a rich syrup'?

Drinkers can enjoy similar contrasts. The open-fired, plush velvet Devonshire Bar serves hand-pulled Tetley Bitter, Foster's lager, Copperhead and Olde English ciders and draught Guinness, to the accompaniment of an old-fashioned Wurlitzer juke box, whilst the exotic cocktail bar, the ceiling of which is decorated with a photographic enlargement of Rubens' *Rape of the Sabine Women*, dispenses the shaken and stirred.

The public bar is open from 11 am to 11 pm. Sunday hours are 12 noon to 10.30 pm. The bistro hours are 9 am to 2 pm and 6 pm to 9.30 pm Monday to Saturday, 9 am to 6 pm on Sunday. Restaurant meals are available every day, lunchtime and evening.

Telephone: 01430 872214.

102

How to get there: The inn is in the centre of Market Weighton, off the A1079 south-east of York.

Parking: Park in the rear car park (through the archway) or on the street.

Length of the walk: 6 miles. OS Map Landranger series 106 (inn GR 878106).

An energetic Wolds Way sampler on tracks and byways, visiting the sites of two medieval villages (Towthorpe and Easthorpe) and Londesborough Park.

The Walk

Turn right from the inn on High Street and walk on past the triple junction, veering right along York Road. Under the street nameplate, across the road, notice the plaque honouring the celebrated Market Weighton giant. Leave the town and, just past the last house, turn right over a stile, following a footpath signposted 'Wolds Way'. Follow the route marked by a line of telegraph poles and continue without deviation along the edges of several fields to the A163.

Cross the road and go straight forward through gates marked 'Towthorpe Grange' on a metalled access road and, passing farm buildings, go through a gate on to pasture land, with the site of Towthorpe village to your left. Swing right, heading for the field corner, and cross the East Beck. Keeping right, cross a stile and follow the line of the beck to the road. Turn left uphill for 100 yards and turn right on a signposted public footpath into Londesborough Park. Continue up a slight incline to the fork and walk on left towards the gate. Just before the gate, turn right over a stile.

I would recommend a short detour here to view the estate buildings and the church of All Saints – go through the gate, take the left fork and go left again opposite the driveway to the hall. Return to the stile to continue the walk.

Drop down to the beck, cross and keep straight forward over the meadow to find a stile in the midway point of a fence. Cross and gradually descend in the direction of a heavily ivied tree in the bottom to the right. The site of Easthorpe village is here. Cross a stile (land liable to flooding), continue over a planked footbridge, cross a second stile and head for a clump of five trees ahead. Maintaining the same line, head for the right-hand corner of a wood and cross a stile to an access road. Turn right along the road, walk on uphill and go left to the next bend. Take the marked footpath to the left and walk on hedgeside to the A163.

Cross, go left 10 yards and turn right on a road, then go left, following a track waymarked 'Wolds Way'. At the field corner, go left along the field edge. On the horizon, the exquisite little village of Goodmanham comes into view. At the field end, take the marked track to the right and, at the corner, go left across a field, downhill to a tunnel, and pass under the embankment of an abandoned railway. Turn right and sharp right again on to the line of the old track and go left, continuing into the outskirts of Market Weighton. Merge with the line of a second track, which joins the footpath from the left, and continue in the direction of the church tower. Swing right and go left opposite Aspen Close on a footpath, merging with Station Road. Go left and turn right along Church Side, then turn left, back to the inn.

Other local attractions: The Market Weighton giant's chair in the Londesborough Arms Hotel (Bradley Room), All Saints church next to the hotel, and an even finer ecclesiastical gem in nearby Goodmanham. Predominantly Norman, this little church succeeds an original structure which was built as a testimony to the conversion of pagan king Coifi to Christianity around AD 625. Inspired by his new-found faith, Coifi dedicated land for the founding of a great cathedral in York.

33 Wetwang
The Black Swan

A Viking expression for a cuff round the lug with a soggy haddock, Wetwang is the name of a village distinguished by a cosy inn which once doubled up as the local fire station. Today the pumps serve only hand-drawn beer, the inn and its distinctive sign looking out on a pond, appropriately cruised by a pair of black swans. Much altered in recent years, the Black Swan has two comfortable front bars, displaying photographs of the old firefighters and a collection of framed tapestries. To the rear is a red velveted snug. A fourth room is available for pool. A pleasant seating/play area behind the inn is ideal for the summer months.

The inn serves John Smith's and a guest beer, Foster's and Kronenbourg lagers, Woodpecker cider and Beamish stout. The standard bar menu includes giant Yorkshire puddings, cottage pie, steak pie, stuffed plaice, pork chops and vegetable lasagne. Specials feature liver and onions, vegetables au gratin and freshly roasted ham in French bread. Sunday lunches are available. The landlady has a reputation for her home-made ice cream. Children have a separate menu.

The Black Swan is open Monday to Friday 11.30 am to 3 pm and

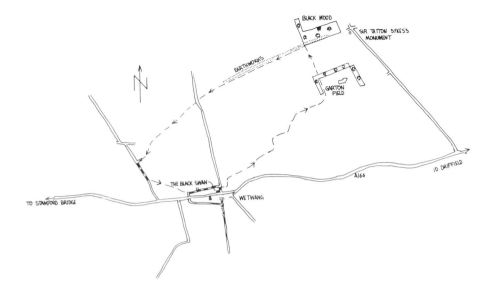

5 pm to 11 pm; Saturday 11 am to 11 pm; Sunday 12 noon to 10.30 pm.
Telephone: 01377 236237.

How to get there: The inn is beside the A166 in the village of Wetwang between Stamford Bridge and Driffield.

Parking: There is only limited parking to the rear. On-street parking is possible as an alternative.

Length of the walk: 6 miles. OS Map Landranger series 106 (inn GR 933592).

Accompanying field edges and furrows, this muddy boots ramble also treads one of the finest green tracks in Yorkshire, a popular route to a stirring monument to Sir Tatton Sykes.

The Walk
(Please note that the 1991 edition of the relevant Ordnance Survey map shows a public right of way which was subsequently diverted by order in 1992. In the early stages of this walk follow the new route markers.)

106

Turn left from the inn and go left by the pond, passing the entrance to a yard on your right (notice the rustic figures?). Walk on for 100 yards and turn right at the Station Hill nameplate, following a sign-posted public footpath. Keep to the field edge and, in the corner, go left downhill. Turn right at the next marker post and continue hedge-side to the end of the field. Drop down to a track and turn right for 10 yards, then go left at the top of the old quarry. Keep going forward across the field to a stile. Cross and swing left and right across a field to a hedge. Go left downhill for 30 yards, turn right at the marker post and go immediately left on the other side of the hedge downhill to the road. (The diversion ends here.)

Turn right along the road to the access to Garton Field. Follow the signposted footpath over a stile here, going diagonally right across the field corner to a gate. Go through, keeping right to the corner and go right hedgeside to a stile. Cross, go left for 20 yards and turn right, continuing until you join a track. Turn left for 100 yards. At the bend, without altering direction, continue, going through double red gates and walking at the edge of a plantation. Walk on, rising to join a green track.

To the right is a prominent landmark, a monument to Sir Tatton Sykes – a 120 ft high Gothic tower, built in 1865, with reliefs on the base showing Sir Tatton on horseback and a country scene.

Turn left for about 1¼ miles to the road. Cross and continue on the track for a further mile or so to the road. Turn left for 400 yards and then left again, following a marked public footpath over a stile. Cross a field, heading for a gate. Go through and cross a meadow, veering right to a gate in the corner. Go through, keep straight forward on a back road, passing bungalows to your right, and continue to Station Hill. Turn right and then right again, back to the inn.

Other local attractions: Church of St Nicholas (Norman fragments), antique shop and craft centre (all in Wetwang).

㉞ Bempton
The White Horse

The true blue virtues of this 1930s brick-built inn extend to the gaily tiled roof, a distinctive landmark, painted black during the war to deceive the Luftwaffe. Little has changed in the intervening years, the White Horse offering a spacious open-fired, part-panelled bar with moquette style seating and an intimate poolroom. There are also two letting bedrooms. The great joy of the inn is its position . . . but it should be renamed. Being only a wing's beat from the famous RSPB sanctuary at Bempton it could be called the Gannet!

The White Horse offers a homely bar menu, listing home-made steak and kidney pie, gammon and pineapple, fried haddock and cod, grilled chicken and various pizzas. Sunday lunches are a speciality. Children are welcome for meals. The house ales include hand-pulled Bass, John Smith's, Timothy Taylor's Landlord, Worthington and Stones, with Kronenbourg and Carling lagers, Autumn Gold and Dry Blackthorn ciders and draught Guinness.

Opening times are Monday, Tuesday and Wednesday 11 am to 4 pm and 7 pm to 11 pm; Thursday, Friday, Saturday and Sunday 11 am to 4.30 pm and 7 pm to 11 pm (10.30 pm on Sunday). Telephone: 01262 850266.

How to get there: The inn is on the B1229 in the village of Bempton, 2½ miles north of Bridlington.

Parking: Park in the inn car park.

Length of the walk: 6½ miles. OS Map Landranger series 101 (inn GR 192722).

Roll up, roll up in April and May for a flying, death defying, squawking, squeaking avian circus, starring breeding gannets, guillemots, kittiwakes, razorbills and puffins. The walk, which is fascinating at any time of year, takes in the RSPB visitor centre (binoculars may be borrowed if car keys are left as a deposit) and the cliffside nesting sites. The return is over pleasant farmland.

The Walk
Turn left from the inn and walk down the road, signposted to the Bempton Bird Sanctuary. Call in at the visitor centre, for details of what's in residence, and go left and right to the cliff path. Turn left and continue past the viewpoints (dangerous cliffs but the edges are stoutly fenced) for about a mile, crossing two stiles. At the third stile, do not cross but go left, following the signpost, 'Buckton 1½ miles'. After ¾ mile, go right and left over two stiles and follow the signpost

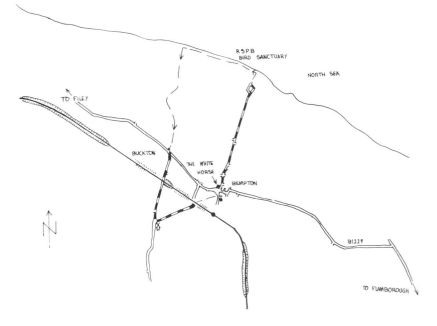

109

to Buckton along Hoddy Cows Lane. Apparently the hoddy cow was a bird like a Norwegian crow which once thrived in the area. The unfortunate creature, which has exotic head plumage reminiscent of a Viking warrior's helmet, is now extremely rare. Please report any sightings to the warden in the visitor centre.

At the road, go left on Main Street and turn right along the quiet Buckton Gate. Continue over the level crossing on Bempton Lane and go next left, following the signpost, 'Bempton 1 mile', on Bolam Lane. Swing left under the railway bridge and go immediately right over a stile, following the signposted footpath to the village green. Aim diagonally left just above the field corner. Cross a second stile, walk over a small meadow and cross a third stile, going left by the village pond and green. Go left again, back to the inn.

Other local attractions: The multiple attractions of the bustling seaside resort of Bridlington to the south.

Stamford Bridge
The Swordsman

Built in the 18th century, serving both the road and river trade, the Swordsman (formerly the New Inn) is sited precariously close to the water, brass plaques affixed to the bar recording the heights of the inundations in 1931 and 1947. Thoroughly modern and with an investment in comfort and amenity extending to both the taproom and the family room, the inn manages to retain its individuality, proudly displaying a collection of Toby jugs, stuffed animals and birds and a gallery of photographs. Its name commemorates the Viking hero of the Battle of Stamford Bridge, fought between King Harold and the Vikings in September 1066, who held the vital bridgehead over the Derwent for hours, singlehanded, atop an ever-growing mound of corpses.

Spear pies were once baked locally in memory of the Saxons' last great victory, but modern invaders can choose from a number of 'Viking Venture' alternatives, with a variety of fillings, including steak, steak and kidney, mince, chicken and sweetcorn and fish. The standard bar menu also features giant Yorkshire puddings, mixed grill, chicken Kiev and grilled steaks. Blackboard specials, served daily, typically include spare ribs, lasagne, chilli con carne and vegetarian

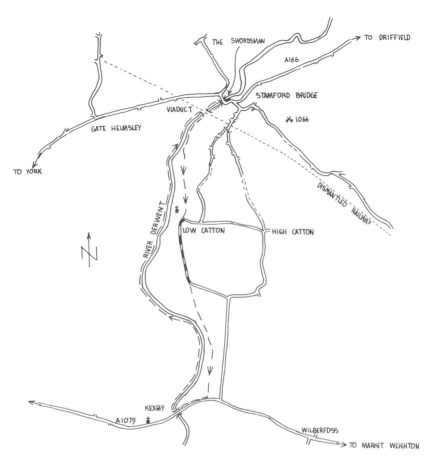

specials such as mushroom and nut fettuccine. Children have their own menu. The house brews are hand-pulled Samuel Smith Old Brewery and Sovereign bitters, Samuel Smith Dark Mild, Ayingerbrau and Ayingerbrau Pils lagers and Cider Reserve. The inn has a pleasant lawned and fenced beer garden to the rear (parents can keep an eye on children from the family room). Day fishing permits are available from the bar (coarse fish and occasional trout).

Opening times are 11 am to 11 pm, Sundays 12 noon to 10.30 pm. In winter (until Easter) the hours on Monday to Thursday are 11 am to 3.30 pm and 5.30 pm to 11 pm).

Telephone: 01759 371307.

How to get there: Adjacent to the single-track bridge over the river, the inn is in Stamford Bridge on the A166 York to Driffield road.

112

Parking: Park in the inn car park.

Length of the walk: 7 miles. OS Map Landranger series 106 (inn GR 712556).

A bridge to bridge, both banks dawdle of the wildlife-rich Derwent.

The Walk

Cross the road in front of the inn and turn right for 20 yards. Go left on Viking Road and immediately turn right, following a public footpath sign on to a picnic area. Go right to the riverbank and turn left along the left bank. Go under the railway viaduct and follow a well-defined path going left of the river over a series of stiles to the village of Low Catton. At the road, swing right through the village, pass the Gold Cup public house and leave the village. At the bend, veer right on a public bridleway between two fields and keep straight ahead hedge and fieldside to the A1079.

Turn right along the footway into Kexby and cross the bridge. At the Humberside sign, turn right on to the right bank of the river. Follow the bank upstream to Stamford Bridge, a distance of some 3½ miles. After passing under the viaduct, veer left to a stile, cross and turn right over the bridge, back to the inn.

Other local attractions: Camping and caravanning close by.

③⑥ Flamborough
The Royal Dog and Duck

A 300-year-old fishermen's inn the house-pets of which were elevated to the peerage in 1900, following the visit of their Serene Highnesses the Prince and Princess Louis of Battenburg, the Royal Dog and Duck can be found in Flamborough's commodious village square. There is more than a whiff of the sea about the jaunty interior, the walls of which are graced by photographs of local craft and by portraits of the gallant salts of the Flamborough lifeboat.

The inn has front and back bars (strike six bells and you would swear you were in the fo'c'sle) a small dining-room and a net-canopied restaurant for evening diners. It also has two patios, one covered. Standard fare, such as traditional steak pie, grilled liver and onions, mixed grill, York ham and roast of the day, is supplemented by seasonal specials like fresh crab, plaice and locally caught cod. And the sweets will also put lead in your sinkers – jam roly-poly and treacle sponge providing strong persuasion to abort this pub walk and to spend a lazy afternoon on the beach. Children are welcome for meals.

The Dog and Duck was once a right royal place for cheap French brandy (in the 18th century the headland was a notorious haunt of smugglers) but today you will need to pay full price for your grog, choosing from hand-pulled Bass, John Smith's, Tetley, Stone's and Worthington bitters, Carling Black Label lager, Autumn Gold and Dry Blackthorn ciders and draught Guinness.

Opening times are Monday to Saturday 11 am to 11 pm. Sunday hours are 12 noon to 10.30 pm.

Telephone: 01262 850206.

How to get there: The inn is in Dog and Duck Square in the centre of the village of Flamborough, 4 miles north-east of Bridlington along the B1255.

Parking: Parking is available in Dog and Duck Square or in the inn car park to the rear.

Length of the walk: 7 miles. OS Map Landranger series 101 (inn GR 227704).

A long, exhilarating roller-coaster circuit of Flamborough Head.

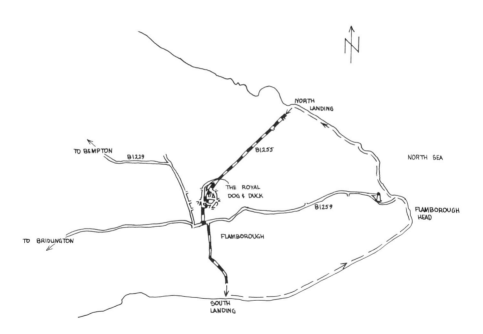

The Walk

Turn right from the inn in Dog and Duck Square, turn right and left, go left again and turn right, following the road signposted to South Landing. Pass the Flamborough Heritage Coast Information Centre (details about local geology, history and wildlife) and continue downhill to South Landing and the sea. Go left up the steps and then right at the top, following the clifftop path.

Swing left to the lighthouse (path diverted because of erosion) and go right by the Headlands Restaurant, turning right to the fire beacon. Go straight forward, following the footpath signposted to North Landing. Turn left past the Caravel Bar overlooking North Landing and, using the roadside footway alongside North Marine Road, walk back into Flamborough. Keep going straight forward along High Street and continue back to the inn.

Other local attractions: North Landing – sandy beach, caves, pleasure trips around the headland and coble (a flat-bottomed boat) fishing. Fresh crabs and lobsters for sale.

37 Laxton
The Bricklayer's Arms

Attesting to the bricklayer's craft inside and out, this backwaters country inn is well worth filling your tank for. In the isolated village of Laxton, within hailing distance of four rivers, the Bricklayer's Arms merrily blends rustication and facilities for modern dining. Traditionalists will stray no further than the open-hearthed bar, furnished with copper-topped tables and bedecked with brasses and horse collars. Formal diners will opt for the waitress service of the purpose-built dining-room.

Standard bar and restaurant fare includes mixed grill, home-made pie of the day, grilled steaks, Yorkshire puddings, halibut and tuna steaks, lemon chicken and vegetarian choices, such as provençal nut Wellington. Sunday lunches are popular and children are welcome for meals. Hand-pulled John Smith's Bitter and Daleside, with Foster's and Becks lagers and draught Guinness are the liquid attractions.

Opening hours are Monday to Friday 7 pm to 11 pm, Saturday 12 noon to 12 midnight and Sunday 12 noon to 3 pm and 7 pm to 10.30 pm.

Telephone: 01430 430111.

117

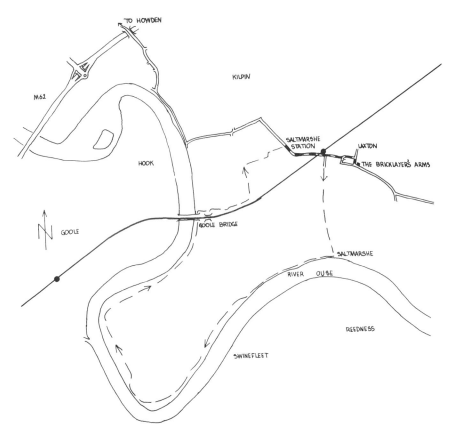

How to get there: The inn is best approached from junction 37 of the M62. Turn right along the A614 for just under 1 mile into Howden and take the next right turn over the motorway, heading south-east for Kilpin, Saltmarshe and Laxton.

Parking: Park in the inn car park.

Length of the walk: 8 miles. OS Map Landranger series 106 (inn GR 790257).

A long, flat, vistas hike in an area which, although only 15 minutes from major conurbations, is as thinly populated as anywhere in Yorkshire. The route hugs the Ouse Bank for over 5 miles. Intent on its course, the river murmurs 'keep your distance', aloof behind its fringe of reeds. With only the wildfowl for company, a cogitative walk for quieter moods.

118

The Walk

Turn right from the inn and go left at the bend for 400 yards, going next left along the road signposted to Saltmarshe. After a mile, turn right at the junction and walk on for 500 yards, going left, following a public footpath sign, through a gate on to the Ouse bank. Go forward, skirting Saltmarshe Hall grounds and continue bankside, swinging round a loop in the river and passing Goole on the far bank, until you come to Goole Bridge (rail). The path is well signposted and is distinct along the whole route.

Turn right at the side of the bridge, dropping off the embankment and going over a stile, and turn left along the road under the bridge, going right at the next junction. Follow the road left and right and, at the next bend, go left of the bridge along the road, swinging left. After walking about 400 yards along the straight, go right, following a direction marker to the edge of a field.

Turn left for 10 yards (deviation from OS map), turn right over a dyke, go left for 20 yards, then turn right, hedgeside, to the road. Turn right, cross the level crossing and walk on, back to the inn.

Other local attractions: Howden, a historic market town with cobbled streets and many fine buildings, the setting for an imposing minster.

Brantingham
The Triton

Triton, son of Poseidon, god of the sea, would be at home in Brantingham. Easy access to the swell, a village pond for tail soaking and a fishy menu at the local pub would have any merman smiling.

The Triton is a thoroughly modern country venue for sophisticated dining, offering a choice of restaurant or bar meals. The pine fittings and pastel shades create a relaxing atmosphere for enjoying an extensive range of bar meals. Piscivores need look no further than the trout, salmon, haddock, halibut, sole and hoki, but the standard menu lists some 40 other choices (plus daily specials), including Yorkshire puddings, mushroom croissant, black pudding, steak and kidney casserole, vegetable macaroni cheese, lamb cutlets, medallions of fillet beef and salmon steak. Sunday lunches are a speciality. Children are welcome for meals and reduced rates are available for senior citizens from Monday to Saturday.

The pampered boot may opt for the swagged opulence of the 70-seater restaurant, indulging in, for example, avocado filled with bacon and tomato sauce topped with smoked cheese and oven baked, and grilled halibut fillet glazed with four cheeses.

The house hand-pulled ales are John Smith's and Theakstons. The complementary brews are Foster's and Kronenbourg lagers and draught Guinness. The inn has a large rear walled beer garden/play area and pleasant seating areas to the front.

Opening times are Monday to Saturday 11.30 am to 2.30 pm and 5.30 pm to 11 pm. On Saturdays between April and September the pub is open from 11 am to 11 pm. Sunday hours are 12 noon to 10.30 pm.

Telephone: 01482 667261.

How to get there: The inn is in the village of Brantingham, off the A63 west of Hull.

Parking: Park in the inn car park.

Length of the walk: 8 miles. OS Map Landranger series 106 (inn GR 939294).

A Wolds Way fields and woodlands circuit, taking in the charms of Welton Dale and Welton village.

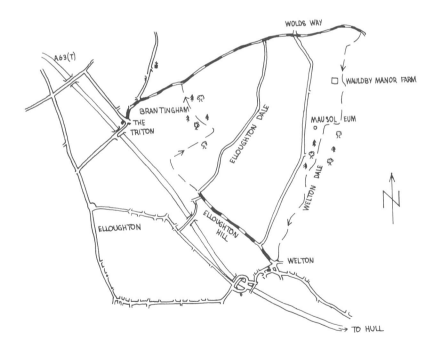

The Walk

Go left from the inn up the steps, cross the road to the war memorial and go left along the road, passing the duckpond. At the bend by the old village pump, go right, following the 'Wolds Way' sign up a steep hill (I knew those profiteroles would have an effect). At the Brantingham Farm access near the top, keep on along a green track to join the road.

Continue along the road for about ¼ mile to the bend and leave the road, veering off right, following a track signposted 'Wolds Way'. Walk on for about ½ mile and turn right by a gate, swinging right and then left along a footpath to Wauldby Manor Farm (the route differs from that shown on the OS map). Going left of the farm, turn left along an access track for 40 yards and go sharp right, following the 'Wolds Way' sign at the side of a pond. Swing right and left alongside first a hedge and then a plantation, and, at the field corner, go briefly into the wood, turning right after 20 yards to follow a path running parallel with the access road.

Continue for 300 yards and go left across the access road, mounting a stile and entering a wood to follow a signposted path. Obscured by trees to the right is a domed classical rotunda built in 1818 by Robert Raikes – a former owner of Welton Hall – as a family mausoleum. Walk on through the wood, leave over a stile and continue at the edge of the plantation, along the floor of lovely Welton Dale. Leave the dale, going through a kissing gate at the side of Dale Cottage and keep forward into the village of Welton.

A detour into Welton is rewarding. The history of the village is colourfully detailed on an information board opposite the pond. The Green Dragon pub opposite is reputed to be the place where the highwayman Dick Turpin was arrested for horse theft in 1759.

Pass Welton Hall and turn right along Kidd Lane. Keep straight on at the T-junction, walking on the vergeside footpath (little traffic) and passing the Elloughton sign. Continue downhill to the junction and turn right, following the road signposted to Elloughton Dale. Go left after 100 yards, off the bend, following a signposted bridleway uphill. Swing right at the crest into the edge of a wood. At the junction of tracks, go left and swing right for 50 yards, then go left, following a public footpath sign, scrambling up a little hill. Weave left and right and go left at the next public footpath sign, down the middle of a narrow wood. Leave the wood, mounting a stile, and go left downhill, retracing your steps back to the inn.

Other local attractions: Humber Bridge and country park (picnic areas and viewpoints) 7 miles south-east.

#

39 **Bielby**
The College Arms

This fashionable country inn was once owned by Merton College, Oxford. Freed from the old school tie, it has since matriculated, losing its alehouse persona in favour of floral prints and red velvet. A retreat for discerning inn-goers, it offers bar and restaurant dining, the standard menu listing a range of steak dishes, chicken in garlic sauce, steak pie, lamb chops, sweet-and-sour pork and fresh haddock. Desserts are of the rib girding kind – treacle and jam roly-poly, spotted dick and various cheesecakes. Children are welcome for meals and there is a snug/games room and a pleasant rear beer garden.

The house bitter is hand-pulled Tetley. The alternative brews are Castlemaine and Lowenbrau lagers and draught Guinness.

Opening times are Monday to Friday 7 pm to 11 pm, Saturday 12 noon to 3 pm and 7 pm to 11 pm and Sunday 12 noon to 3 pm and 7 pm to 10.30 pm.

Telephone: 01759 318361.

How to get there: The inn is in the village of Bielby, south of Pocklington and the A1079.

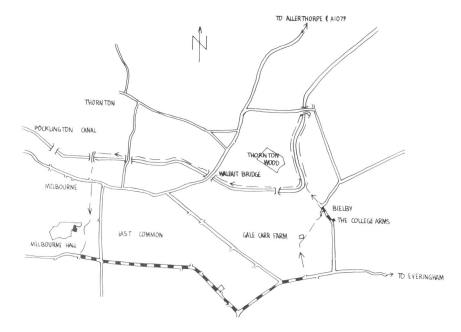

Parking: Park in the car park to the rear.

Length of the walk: 8 miles. OS Map Landranger series 106 (inn GR 791437).

A peek-a-boo nature ramble along the Pocklington Canal, returning along country tracks and lanes . . . wildfowl, rooks, a tribute to Bomber Command and what must be one of the biggest sundials in the world.

The Walk

Turn right from the inn, along the road. Pass the church and, at the bend, keep forward on a metalled road to the Bielby Beck. Cross on a bridge, and veer right, following a marked public footpath alongside the cut. On reaching the side of the canal, turn right and walk on, bankside, to a bridge. Go left over the bridge and then left again, walking along the opposite bank of the canal, continuing for about 1 ¾ miles to Walbut Bridge. Walk on, beside the canal, for a further ¾ mile to a bridge. Continue canalside for ⅓ mile to a bridge and turn left, passing a marina, on a track to the road and the village of Melbourne.

Turn right for 20 yards along the road and go left down St Monica's Close. Go left at the top of the close, veering left of the church and

124

cross a stile and a planked bridge over a ditch, going forward on a footpath marked by a line of telegraph poles. Keep straight forward at the last pole (they veer off right), cross a stile and a narrow field and cross another stile to an access. Go left for 10 yards and turn right, following yellow route markers, up the driveway to Melbourne Hall (blessed with a raucous rookery). Just before the drive enters the grounds, go left by the metal gate, following the direction marker, aiming diagonally left to bisect the field into the far corner. Turn right, again following the route marker, and go down the middle of the field, aiming right of the farmhouse gable to a stile and the road.

Turn left along the road for about 1 ½ miles. You will pass an old wartime airfield on the right (stop to inspect the tribute to the comrades of Bomber Command) and an amazing mammoth sundial on the frontage of Dial Hall Farm.

At the road junction, turn left, following the signpost to Bielby. At the next junction, swing right on the road signposted to Everingham. Walk on for 500 yards and go left, following a marked public footpath, over a stile and a planked bridge and going hedgeside to the field corner. Cross a second planked bridge, following the route marker straight forward across a field to the right of a farmhouse. Go right on a track, following a line of telegraph poles, and swing left to the entrance to Gale Carr Farm. Turn right here, following the direction sign along a track to Bielby church. Turn right, back to the inn.

Other local attractions: Fishing and boating on the Pocklington Canal.

④⓪ Kilnsea
The Crown and Anchor

Protected by a pill-box against an enemy who never came, the most easterly inn in the United Kingdom has crow's-nest views of the Humber. If the watchwords are Location! Location! Location! this uniquely situated pub has everything. Thoroughly modernised in recent years, it is full of character, having open fires and stoned flagged floors, its walls acting as a gallery for local artists works – paintings and photographs adorning its walls. It has an attractive dining room, four letting en suite bedrooms and a rear beer garden.

Tuck in, while you scan the sea lanes from this comfortable pub, and enjoy something from the range of steak dishes, home-made soups and pies – fish and steak and ale – and fresh fish. The bar dispenses hand-pulled Tetley and Calder's bitter, Tetley dark mild, and Carlsberg lager.

Opening times are 11 am to 11 pm (10.30 pm on Sundays) in season. During the winter months opening times vary according to the number of customers who can beat a salty path to its door!

Telephone: 01964 650276.

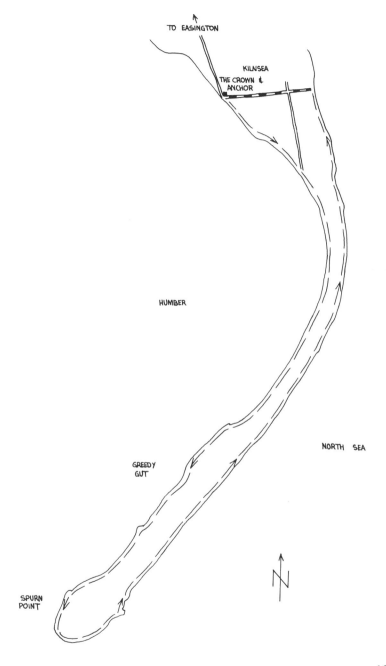

TO EASINGTON

KILNSEA

THE CROWN &
ANCHOR

HUMBER

NORTH SEA

GREEDY
GUT

N

SPURN
POINT

127

How to get there: Drive to the southerly extremity of Yorkshire and the inn is the last licensed landfall before you need a propellor. Take the B1445 fork in Patrington and go through Easington to the hamlet of Kilnsea – only 20 yards from the Humber bank.

Parking: Park in the inn car park.

Length of the walk: 8½ miles. OS Map Landranger series 113 (inn GR 409158).

Yorkshire sticks its tongue out at an eternally fretful North Sea and pays for its impudence in gnawings and frequent breaches. Visiting the mysteriously shifting Spurn spit, this immensely interesting walk is a must for botanists and ornithologists. Dogs are prohibited in the nature reserve in order to protect the wildlife.

The Walk
Turn left from the inn along the raised footpath, go through a gate and turn right on the road for 100 yards to the Spurn Nature Reserve access sign. Continue along the public footpath, walking either on the footpath, the road or along the shoreline to the point.

The lifeboat station near the head is manned by a full-time professional crew. Notice the sites of old lighthouses and the vain attempts at tide containment. Broken lamp standards, demolition debris – everything and the kitchen sink is used in the relentless battle with the sea. Some say the fight is already lost and Spurn will shortly disappear, so come soon.

Return, going north on the seaward side. Just before the Kilnsea caravan park, go left along the road and walk back to the inn.

Other local attractions: Being the first landfall for rare migrant birds, Spurn attracts large numbers of twitchers. Hides are provided. Bring binoculars.